Fingerplays and the Science of Reading in Early Childhood

Unlock the magic of fingerplays and transform your early childhood classroom with this essential guide bridging research and practice.

While many books compile fingerplays and action rhymes, few explore their rich history or the science behind their impact on early literacy and social development. This groundbreaking guide offers teachers and caregivers a resource that connects tradition with evidence-based practices, examining how fingerplays align with the latest research in the science of reading and offering insights into their effectiveness.

Featuring a wealth of research on early literacy and social development, the book includes a practical section filled with selected rhymes and visual cues for easy classroom implementation. *Fingerplays and the Science of Reading in Early Childhood* is a timeless addition to any early childhood educator's collection.

Meghan Dunne Raderstrong is a teacher in White Plains, New York, where she uses her passion for literacy to help her students develop and grow as readers. She has been teaching young children for 15 years in the classroom, as a reading specialist and by supporting multilingual learners. Holding a degree in Early Childhood Education and Literacy, as well as a TESOL advanced certificate, Meghan uses her expertise in language acquisition to create inclusive and engaging learning experiences for all students. She and her family live among the legends in Sleepy Hollow, NY.

Also Available from Routledge
Eye on Education
www.routledge.com/k-12

Reimagining the Role of Teachers in Nature-based Learning:
Helping Children be Curious, Confident, and Caring
Rachel Larimore and Claire Warden

Promoting Language and Early Literacy Development:
Practical Insights from a Parent Researcher
Pamela Beach

Teaching Higher-Order Thinking to Young Learners, K–3:
How to Develop Sharp Minds for the Disinformation Age
Steffen Saifer

Everyday STEAM for the Early Childhood Classroom:
Integrating the Arts into STEM Teaching
Margaret Loring Merrill

A New Vision for Early Childhood: Rethinking Our
Relationships with Young Children
Noah Hichenberg

Fingerplays and the Science of Reading in Early Childhood

How the Tradition of Action Rhymes Can Support Emerging Readers

Meghan Dunne Raderstrong

Routledge
Taylor & Francis Group

NEW YORK AND LONDON

Designed cover image: Getty Images.

First published 2025
by Routledge
605 Third Avenue, New York, NY 10158

and by Routledge
4 Park Square, Milton Park, Abingdon, Oxon, OX14 4RN

Routledge is an imprint of the Taylor & Francis Group, an informa business

© 2025 Meghan Dunne Raderstrong

The right of Meghan Dunne Raderstrong to be identified as author of this work has been asserted in accordance with sections 77 and 78 of the Copyright, Designs and Patents Act 1988.

All rights reserved. No part of this book may be reprinted or reproduced or utilised in any form or by any electronic, mechanical, or other means, now known or hereafter invented, including photocopying and recording, or in any information storage or retrieval system, without permission in writing from the publishers.

Trademark notice: Product or corporate names may be trademarks or registered trademarks, and are used only for identification and explanation without intent to infringe.

Library of Congress Cataloging-in-Publication Data
Names: Raderstrong, Meghan author
Title: Fingerplays and the science of reading in early childhood : how the tradition of action rhymes can support emerging readers / Meghan Raderstrong.
Description: New York, NY : Routledge, 2025. | Series: Routledge eye on education | Includes bibliographical references.
Identifiers: LCCN 2024062021 (print) | LCCN 2024062022 (ebook) | ISBN 9781032986418 (hardback) | ISBN 9781032986401 (paperback) | ISBN 9781003599746 (ebook)
Subjects: LCSH: Reading (Early childhood) | Finger play. | English language--Study and teaching (Early childhood)--Foreign speakers.
Classification: LCC LB1139.5.R43 R33 2025 (print) | LCC LB1139.5.R43 (ebook) | DDC 372.4--dc23/eng/20250319
LC record available at https://lccn.loc.gov/2024062021
LC ebook record available at https://lccn.loc.gov/2024062022

ISBN: 978-1-032-98641-8 (hbk)
ISBN: 978-1-032-98640-1 (pbk)
ISBN: 978-1-003-59974-6 (ebk)

DOI: 10.4324/9781003599746

Typeset in Palatino
by KnowledgeWorks Global Ltd.

Dedication

For all our young children, especially my own.
Oscar and Elias: I love watching your brains, and hearts, grow.

Table of Contents

Acknowledgments..................................viii

Introduction...................................1

1 The Science of Reading............................10

2 The Magic of Rhymes 23

3 Beyond Literacy................................39

4 In Practice..................................54

5 Rhyming with Language Learners 69

6 The Rhymes..................................76

Acknowledgments

In 2023, I returned to teaching after COVID and a long maternity leave, committed to centering what I loved about education. I decided I would follow whatever made me excited and brought joy to my days as a teacher. I incorporated more play and novelty and brought in items, books, and rhymes from my children at home. I remained committed to my passion for and belief in evidence-driven practices and was constantly on the lookout for places where joy and evidence overlapped.

To all the teachers I have worked alongside: thank you for sharing your ideas, thoughts, and worries. Thank you for spending your time thinking about, planning for, and working with children. I have learned so much from the wonderful people I have worked alongside. Let's keep finding the joy in teaching and holding it tight.

I am grateful for my parents, who helped raise my sisters and I to love books, stories and sounds. To my mom who encouraged our reading with the best books and nightly read alouds, and my dad who was playing phonological awareness games without even realizing it. Thank you "som uch."

I had the idea for this book, and my wonderful husband encouraged me to just sit down and write. I was shocked, by both how easily the idea took form and how much I enjoyed it. Jeff, thank you for always encouraging me. You are truly the most incredible partner I could ask for. Thank you for lending your professional expertise to this book and for creating the space for me to write it.

And to Oscar and Elias. You made me a mother, and for that, I am eternally grateful. Becoming your mother fundamentally changed my perspective as a teacher, and watching you grow has taught me more about little humans than I could have ever learned from a book. I hope that your lives continue to be full of love and good books.

Introduction

I remember practicing the "Open and Shut Them" rhyme in the mirror the night after my first day as a teacher. I was teaching a pre-kindergarten class of 25 four-year-old students and the first day was full of tears, play dough bits squished into the floor, and many, many assisted bathroom breaks. That day, I had somehow successfully dropped them off for lunch and was walking by another classroom. From inside, I heard the veteran teacher start to sing: "Open shut them, open shut them." I couldn't resist peeking in. What I saw blew my mind: all of the kindergarteners quickly gathered around the teacher on the carpet, eyes glued to her hands, hanging on every word she sang. As soon as she finished the rhyme, she repeated it once more, and almost all of the students joined in, mimicking her hand movements and even chiming in with some of the words. As soon as she finished the second time, she opened up a book and began to read. The students, hands in laps as the rhyme directed, were rapt. After experiencing the tornado of my morning, I could not believe what I had seen. It was like magic.

On my second day of school, after dutifully practicing what I had seen the day before, we finished eating breakfast, and I called the students to the rug. About half of my class came right over, and the rest were throwing garbage away, bobbing around the edge of the carpet, or some combination of the two. Channeling my inner veteran teacher, I began the rhyme. "Open shut them, open shut them…"

My voice started off shaky, but stabilized as I observed the eyes of my students quickly settle on me, and some little hands begin to open and shut as well. "Give a little clap!" Now even the attention of my students bobbing around was on the carpet, and most began moving toward us. "Open shut them, open shut them…" Then, all of the students were on the carpet, opening and closing their little fists, leaning gently toward me. "Place them in your lap!" I was shocked to see the busy fingers find their little laps, looking eagerly at me to see what came next. I repeated the

DOI: 10.4324/9781003599746-1

rhyme, now with all students in front of me, and launched right into my morning read aloud as soon as we finished.

I was pleasantly surprised to find that I pulled off this magic. I didn't know it then, but what I had experienced was something that teachers had been practicing for generations. Action rhymes and fingerplays have been in use in early childhood classrooms for hundreds of years. These rhymes are shared from teacher to teacher or picked up from an old book discovered in school libraries or a childhood bookshelf. Some teacher training programs, if you were very lucky, would incorporate them as a tool to use in your classrooms, but mostly the magic of these rhymes was something that felt alive. Passed along the hallways, recalled from your own childhood, heard on the playground, or picked up in your baby's music class. Teachers are used to learning from one another, and often this kind of peer sharing is the best way to develop your toolbox of on-the-ground strategies.

As I continued in early elementary classrooms, fingerplays and rhymes became central to my student's experience. We collected these rhymes over the school year, adding in a new one after many repetitions of previous rhymes left them permanently stored in our minds. We would recite them in different voices, impersonating Papa Bear after reading *Goldilocks and the Three Bears*, and Piggie after reading Mo Willems. We had posters with images cuing us to each rhyme, and students took turns selecting and leading their peers. Students repeated the rhymes to younger siblings and parents, and soon other teachers stopped outside my door to see what it was that had my students so engaged. For years, the magic of reciting rhymes with motion felt like just that: magic. It wasn't until recently that I learned it is more than magic… It is science.

I am now a reading specialist and English as a New Language (ENL) teacher. With a master's degree in both early childhood and literacy, you would think I had learned about the science of reading in my training. However, like many of us, it was a podcast that changed the trajectory of my teaching. In August 2019, a colleague and friend sent me Emily Hanford's audio documentary "At a Loss for Words." I listened to the episode the week before we had to return to school as I was in my classroom unpacking boxes and experimenting with different room layouts. I had the documentary playing on my speakers as I dragged my carpet from spot to spot in my classroom, looking for the right place to make magic with my incoming students. What I heard completely changed my approach to teaching reading. So many of the practices I had learned from my teacher preparation programs, practices I used every day in my classroom, had little to no evidence behind them. Like the fingerplays, they were also passed from classroom to classroom, yet instead of creating magic, these practices left us unequipped to teach all students to read. Unlike the fingerplays, these practices had been actively taught to us in graduate class, week-long district professional development, and in published resources, we purchased with our own money to read over the summer. I left my school that day in distress – how did this happen, and how quickly could I catch up?

I became obsessed with learning about evidence-based reading instruction. For months, the only content I read, listened to, and discussed (sometimes with my patient but not completely interested family and friends) was about reading instruction. I learned that phonological awareness instruction was the foundation on which all reading instruction is built. While I had been teaching phonics for years, I learned that the strategies I used in my guided reading groups could undermine the systematic phonics programs I worked so hard to implement. So many of us were led to believe that, after a certain amount of guided reading, independent practice, and leveled books, somehow magic would happen and children would learn to read. The science now shows this magic doesn't exist. I became an advocate for evidenced-based practices in my district, sharing resources and curriculum with other teachers and my administration. When COVID sent us home in March 2020, I began developing training on phonological awareness over Zoom. By the time we were back (part-time, in person) in September 2020, it became clear that we had no time to waste with our students. Every minute must be spent wisely.

I used this sense of urgency to examine each of my classroom practices, making sure that there was science behind each of the instructional choices I made. This critical lens replaced many of my long-standing teacher moves. I took down my posters about picture support and reorganized my leveled texts by content and theme. I wrote grants for decodable books and dusted off old manipulatives to use for phonemic awareness exercises. As I looked at my key ring full of fingerplay cue cards, I had to ask myself... Science, or magic? In the case of fingerplays, the answer is both.

Research vs. Practice

Unfortunately, too few teachers have been given the opportunity to explore the science behind their practice and instead just follow the lead of their district's chosen curriculum without broader reflection on evidence-based practices. Why is that? One of the reasons is that we are so busy throughout our day.

Let us consider just the first part of a kindergarten teacher's day.

It is 7:20 am and you flip on the lights in your classroom. The rug still has vacuum marks from the custodial crew's work the evening before, and you enter trying to decide where to begin. Student laughter and stories will start pouring in the door by 8:20, so you prioritize. You take the chairs down from the tables, and set out morning baskets full of table toys you found on Facebook Marketplace and drove a half an hour to collect, then cleaned and sorted for your students to use. You change the daily calendar, adjust the classroom jobs, and then begin to write your learning objectives on your board, referring to your planbook for all the different skills "students will be able to" do after today. You place your sticky notes with preplanned higher-order questions in your read aloud for the day, intentionally planning how you will ask each question to monitor for understanding across your entire class. You take five minutes to check your emails, looking for announcements from your principal about where your class will place for recess today and for any updated dismissal plans for this afternoon. You are just able to finish writing the morning message on your chart paper as the kids come running in. You attempt to turn your lesson manuals to the right pages and place them near your spot on the carpet but are frequently interrupted for hugs, to hear about lost teeth and little siblings, and to help students with stuck zippers or opening milk cartons.

Needless to say, the day does not slow down once your room is full of five- and six-year-olds. The life of a classroom teacher is fast paced, demanding, and a lot of fun. Early childhood educators, especially, are not only responsible for academic instruction but for all the care tasks that come along with teaching young children. While we are excited to teach reading, we are also tasked with teaching things like cutting with scissors, cleaning up messes, tying shoes, taking turns, and giving hugs and bandages after a fall on the playground. It is a messy and beautiful job, and most early childhood educators cannot imagine spending their life in any other way.

Through all these small tasks, teachers have a direct, daily impact on the students they teach. They can influence the way these students go on to interact with their communities beyond the classroom. Great leaders across many fields cite a specific teacher as the reason they decided to pursue their path. We have all been shaped by the teachers who have stood beside us as we learned as children and beyond. And of all the things that we learn, learning to read is undoubtedly the most foundational. Learning to read allows us to access infinite knowledge. In fact, once it is assumed that students know how to read, we begin to expect them to learn much of the other content areas *through* reading. That means that we, as early childhood educators, are responsible for teaching the most foundational skill in the most foundational job.

The people who are tasked with understanding the science behind learning – educational researchers – also have a very important job. They are responsible for uncovering essential information about how we learn.

Their day, however, looks much different than that of a teacher. Most educational researchers are also professors, and while their work with college and graduate students will keep them busy, their classrooms are not as involved as the early childhood educators. Which is good, because they have their hands full with more than just teaching. They conduct important studies, collect evidence, analyze their data, and spend countless hours crafting their findings into articles that will go on to be reviewed and hopefully published by field-defining publications. Furthermore, reading research transcends traditional academic departments, spanning across subdisciplines in psychology, linguistics, neuroscience.

And while the work of researcher and teacher is, in many ways, dependent on one another, quite rarely do the two actually interact. Traditionally, the work of education researchers is published in academic journals or presented at industry conferences. There are think tanks and nonprofits committed to furthering research on content acquisition, teaching methods, school innovation, and more. Sometimes researchers collaborate with these organizations to help put on conferences or roundtables to discuss their latest findings and the implications on teaching and learning.

I remember my first year teaching. I was on the mailing list for one of these organizations. They had an upcoming discussion about a new study on phonemic awareness that was just published. I was so excited to learn more about it, but when I went to register, I saw the event was from 12:00 to 1:00 pm. Ironically, I would be teaching my literacy block at that time.

This kind of conflict is understandable. While researchers want the information they discover and publish to be accessible to those in schools teaching, the structures through which they share information are often not easy for full-time classroom teachers to access. We are not the intended participants for the conferences, even when the keynote speaker is reporting on research done with the curriculum we use every day. And while teachers work every single day to make sure they are effectively teaching their students, their time is largely spent with the 25 children who walk through their doors every morning, and not shifting through the research journals or attending conferences.

So, how do we expect teachers to know the most up-to-date research on how children learn to read? We may hope that teacher preparation programs are equipping our teachers-to-be with this information, but a study done in 2023 by the National Council on Teacher Quality found that only 25% of education preparation programs adequately address all five core components of reading instruction (Ellis et al., 2023, p.9). Even if these programs currently make adjustments to their curriculum, which many are, it means that there are hundreds of thousands of teachers who have already graduated who were not given access to the essential information about how to teach reading. We may hope that the curriculum districts purchase to guide their teacher's time with students would align with the most up-to-date research on reading, but unfortunately, that is not the case. Emily Hanford's (2022) podcast "Sold a Story" documents how one incorrect idea about reading has persisted in reading curriculums across the country, causing many programs to build reading instruction around an idea that was debunked by reading researchers. Teachers are required to implement district-provided curriculums and, never having been taught about the reading research that exists, have no reason to question it.

I know this story well, because I am one of these teachers. Despite having two master's and three teaching certifications, frequently listening to podcasts about education on my drive to work, often stacking my summer reading with texts about how students learn, and signing up for every professional development webinar I could get my hands on, I taught for almost ten years before I knew how robust the research reading acquisition was. As well as how misaligned it was with what I was doing in my classroom each day.

I hope that this book can be one small bridge between the research of education and the practice of teaching. I also hope it can be a model for how to use existing research on best practices to reflect on classroom practice to ensure it aligns with the evidenced-based body of literature on how to effectively educate children. By presenting the research on the science of reading – which still has not been absorbed by as many early childhood educators as it should be – I will give you a foundation to understand not only how humans learn to read, but also to see how to use this knowledge to reflect on long-held classroom practices. And, with this foundation in place, the book will also share how fingerplays can be used in a way that supports this kind of evidence-based learning, each and every day in your classroom.

First, I will summarize some of the most applicable information from the body of research we call The Science of Reading. I believe knowing this information is essential for all educators, especially early childhood educators who are teaching foundational reading skills every day. Then I will explain the recommendations for teaching that come from a review of this literature and demonstrate how the incorporation of rhymes supports building important pathways for foundational reading skills. Then I will venture beyond reading, discussing the role fingerplays play in developing self-regulation and auditory comprehension. Finally, I will explore ways to use them in your classroom, including an appendix of fingerplays, collected from other classrooms, library story times, vintage books, children's music classes, and the memories of my own childhood. I provide you with images for each and demonstrate how you can make them a part of the magic you are making each and every day.

Teaching reading is the most essential role early childhood teachers play. Teachers are working hard on the ground every day, using resources from curricula, fellow teachers, and their years of studying in educational programs. I know there *is* magic happening in each of our classrooms, and now we can point to a body of scientific research to better understand why.

Handy Highlights

- ☞ Fingerplays are an old practice, not frequently taught to teachers, but passed down from educator to educator.
- ☞ Many teachers have not been taught the science of reading and may use non-research-backed curricula to help students learn.
- ☞ Understanding how we learn to read is essential for all early childhood educators. It will shape how we teach early readers.
- ☞ Fingerplays can be an evidence-aligned compliment to a teacher's literacy instruction.

References

Ellis, C., Holston, S., Drake, G., Putman, H., Swisher, A., & Peske, H. (2023). *Teacher prep review: Strengthening elementary reading instruction*. National Council on Teacher Quality.

Hanford, E. (Host). (n.d.). Sold a Story [Audio podcast]. American Public Media. https://features.apmreports.org/sold-a-story/

1

The Science of Reading

As Louisa Moats wrote, teaching children to read *is* rocket science (2020). Unfortunately, learning to read has not always been treated as such. As I shared in the last chapter, many teachers have historically been provided materials and information that make it seem like with enough exposure to print and love for reading, learning to read will occur, just like magic.

Because there are few things more important in our modern society than learning how to read, we deserve better. Teachers and families need access to the information about how humans learn how to read, and children should have teachers who know how to act on this information to help transform them into fluent readers.

To help support a better understanding of how we all learn how to read, this chapter will summarize some of the most relevant research that makes up "The Science of Reading." While this chapter is the only one in the book that does not directly reference fingerplays, it is an important foundation for the chapters to come. Without an understanding of the science of reading, we cannot understand how fingerplays serve both as science and magic in our classrooms. After this chapter lays this foundation, the remaining chapters will build from it to show how early childhood educators can use fingerplays as an evidence-driven practice in their classroom.

The Reading League, an organization whose mission is to advance the understanding and use of evidence-aligned reading instruction through the science of reading, gives us a definition of the science of reading:

> The science of reading is a vast, interdisciplinary body of scientifically-based research about reading and issues related to reading and writing.
>
> This research has been conducted over the last five decades across the world, and it is derived from thousands of studies conducted in multiple languages. The science of reading has culminated in a preponderance of evidence to inform how proficient reading and writing develop; why some have difficulty; and how we can most effectively assess and teach and, therefore, improve student outcomes through prevention of and intervention for reading difficulties.
>
> The Reading League (TRL) (2022)

I will summarize the most relevant information from this body of research to show how our brains change as we learn to read, as well as different models for understanding how we learn this essential skill.

Changing Brains

Almost all children who can hear will learn to talk without formal instruction. Except for those with severe developmental disabilities, learning to speak is a natural process that happens with exposure to speech and language. The human brain has evolved over many years to support this natural acquisition of language.

Reading, however, is not a natural process. Written language systems are a more "recent" invention, only beginning to show up in societies 12–15 thousand years ago (Dehaene, 2009). Because written language is newer than spoken language, our brains have not had a chance to adapt and rewire to make reading happen naturally. That said, everyone is capable of *learning* to read. So, what happens in our brains to overcome this challenge?

Over the last few decades, advances in technology have been able to provide us with the tools to study this exact question. Functional magnetic resonance imaging (fMRI) allows for the study of the brain while it completes different reading-related tasks. Along with the measurement of eye movement and reaction times, this type of measurement has taught researchers a great deal about how the brain is rewired to acquire the ability to read.

The brain is a complex organ, with several regions that are responsible for a variety of tasks. By observing which regions of the brain are active during different tasks, we are able to see how the brain makes meaning from print. When you speak a word aloud, an area on the left side of your brain which is responsible for processing speech sounds is activated. When you are just speaking a word without reading it, only that area responsible for processing speech lights up.

Now consider what happens when someone is given a written word to read. When someone is given a written word, imaging shows that the area in the back of the brain that processes visual information is activated. If this person has never been taught to read, this is where the activation ends. However, in brain scans of those who have been taught to read, something amazing happens. Instead of the activation ending there, researchers see the brain's activity connect from the visual processing area in the back of the brain to the speech processing area on the left side of the brain. This shows that a written word actually triggers the speech processing area of our brain, even when the word is not read aloud (Amplify Education, 2018).

Between the visual processing zone at the back of the brain and the speech processing zone on the left side is what is called the "visual word form area." If you have learned to read, you have this area in your brain. If you have not learned to read, you do not. Stanislas Dehaene, in his seminal book *Reading in the Brain*, calls this area "The Brain's Letterbox," since this is the area that deals with the recognition and connection of letters to sounds. We can observe that humans are born with the language part of their brain that allows for the natural acquisition of speech. And we know that we are born with a visual processing area that allows us to process faces, shapes, and objects. That said, no one is born with the connections between these two areas, which is essential for reading. We actually have to build this "letterbox," one connection between visual information and sound (such as learning that the letter m makes the sound/m/) at a time. Every word that is read is a product of connecting visually recognized letters and letter sequences to the sounds of spoken words, a process called **orthographic mapping** (Moats & Tolman, 2019). It is through orthographic mapping that we build our "letterbox" and learn how to read.

Another important finding is that we do not read print selectively, skipping over words or letters while we read. Though whole language theorists once thought this to be true, each time we read a word we are actually processing each individual letter. This is what allows us to distinguish between words that look similar but have different meanings, like the words addition and audition. Eye movement studies have confirmed that skilled readers aren't skipping words or guessing at what words are based on context. Even though skilled readers may feel like they are able to recognize a word instantly, research has shown that they are processing each individual letter and its connection to speech (Moats & Tolman, 2019).

The Four-Part Processing Model was created as a way to represent these complex processes (Seidenberg & McClelland, 1989). While it is a simplification of the exact mechanisms in our brains, it is a useful way to demonstrate the complexity of mental activity happening while we read. It illustrates that reading is dependent on created pathways in the language and visual processing areas of our brain (Figure 1.1).

As Moats and Tolman (2019) explain, this model shows how all of these processing systems work together in fluent reading and reminds us of the importance of teaching to each one. The **phonological processing system** is responsible for a remarkable number of essential tasks, including producing speech sounds, remembering and repeating words, holding sounds in working memory to allow for writing them down, and producing

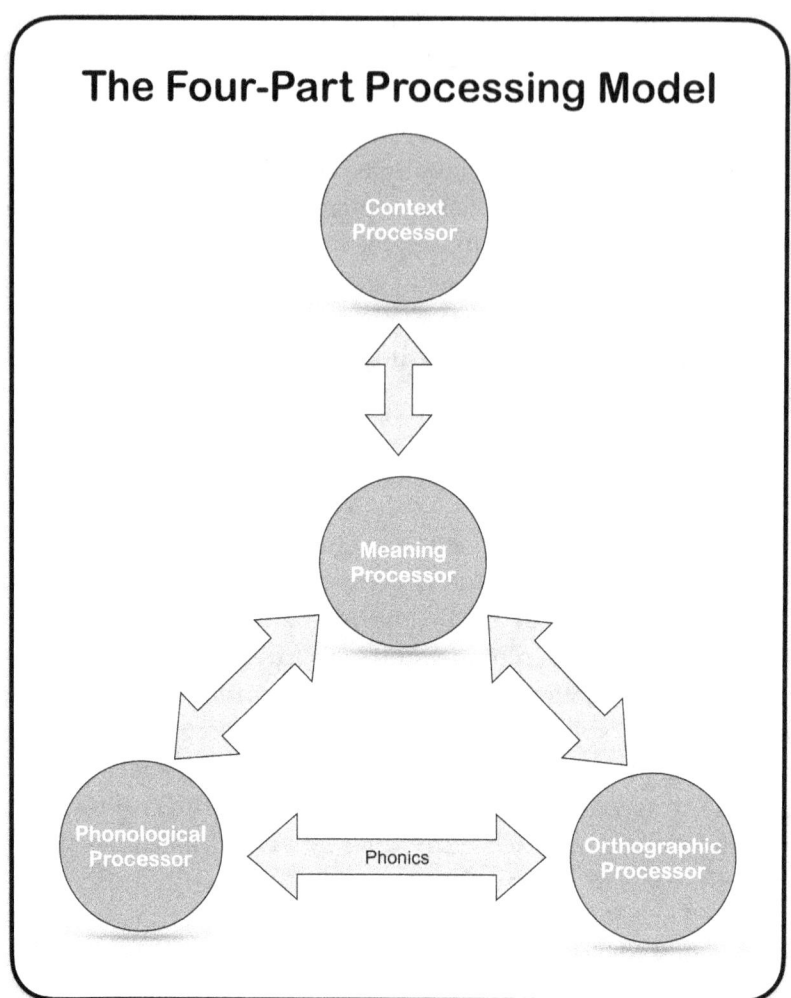

FIGURE 1.1 The Four-Part Processing Model (Seidenberg & McClelland, 1989)

phrasing and prosody in speech. When it comes to reading, the phonological processing system is responsible for the critical work of phonemic awareness. A **phoneme** is the smallest unit of sounds in a language, such as the sound the letter g makes in the word bug. Phonemic awareness is the ability to identify, hear, and manipulate the individual phonemes within spoken words. This is crucial for learning to read and spell, which requires the connection of individual sounds to letters or letter combinations.

The **orthographic processing system** includes the "brain's letterbox," but is also responsible for broader functions related to recognition and recall of written language symbols such as the quick retrieval of letter and letter sequences to allow for fluent decoding and spelling. The orthographic processing system allows us to recognize letter forms in different handwriting or fonts.

The **meaning processing system** is the area in our brain where we connect a word to what it represents. This area is responsible for our understanding of what words mean and their relationship to one another. It creates mental images of words. The mental image becomes sharper with more exposure to the word and its various forms. Think about the first time you hear a new word. You may be able to understand it enough to make sense of it; however, you may not feel comfortable using it on your own. The more exposure you have, the more the meaning processing system can clarify the meaning, eventually leaving you confident in how to use it.

Finally, the **context processing system** supports the meaning processing system. This system is commonly used as we attempt to assign meaning to a word based on context. This is helpful when dealing with homophones, words that sound the same but are spelled differently, and heteronyms, words that are spelled the same but pronounced differently.

This model helps us to organize the information we have about what is happening in the brain when we read. The next section will focus on *The Simple View of Reading*, which builds on what is happening in the brain and emphasizes the measurable skills required to be a skilled reader.

The Simple View of Reading

The intentional building of our brain's "letterbox" is only one part of what makes for successful reading. In 1986, psychologists Philip Gough and William Tunmer proposed that reading comprehension, which is the ultimate goal of any reader, is the product of printed word recognition and language

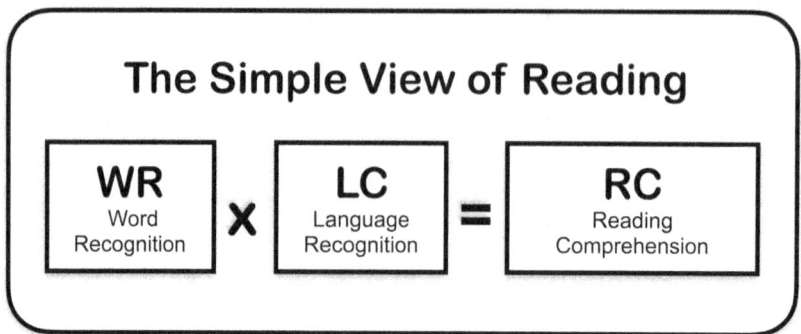

FIGURE 1.2 The Simple View of Reading (Gough & Turner, 1986)

comprehension. They called this theory **The Simple View of Reading** (Figure 1.2).

The factors in this equation are word recognition and language comprehension. Word recognition refers to the accurate and fast retrieval of words in print. This is the work happening in our brain's "letterbox," that we described in the previous section.

ძალიან კარგი მკითხველი ვარ

This sentence is written in Georgian. While the sentence is simple in its meaning, if you are unable to decode the letters, matching them to sounds and therefore forming meaningful words, you cannot understand what the sentence means. When we teach phonics, our goal is to help students build a letterbox that allows for the quick and accurate retrieval of decoded words. In order to sufficiently develop word recognition, students need strong phonological awareness, phonics, and fluency skills.

The second factor in the equation is language comprehension. Language comprehension refers to the ability to make meaning from spoken words. This may be measured by reading a passage aloud to a student and then having them retell important information from the passage and answer questions about it. Italian and English both use the Latin alphabet. This means that they largely share the same basic set of letters, though some accents or sound pronunciation may vary.

Sono un ottimo lettore

This sentence is written in Italian. You may be able to decode and pronounce the words written there (though likely with an accent most Italians would chuckle at); however, if you do not know the meaning of the words, you will not understand the sentence. This also applies when, even if you speak the language, you don't understand the terms being used.

> Suppose we have two quits. If these were two classical bits, then there would be four possible states, 00, 01, 10, and 11. Correspondingly, a two qubit system has four computational basis states denoted $|00\rangle, |01\rangle, |10\rangle, |11\rangle$. A pair of qubits can also exist n superpositions of these four states, so the quantum state of two qubits involves associating a complex coefficient - sometimes called an amplitude - with each computational basis state, such that the state vector describing the two qubits is...
>
> Nielsen and Chuang (2010)

Unless you are well-versed in quantum computation, you were likely able to decode the words in this passage but unable to comprehend what it was attempting to convey.

The theory suggests that you can predict how well a student comprehends what they read by multiplying a measure of their ability to decode words by a measure of their ability to understand spoken language. Notably, the theory uses multiplication, not addition, as the mathematical operation in this equation. That means, if either factor is zero (meaning, they neither decode words or understand the spoken language), the subject's overall ability to comprehend reading will be zero as well. For all three of the examples I provided above, either my ability to decode the words or my ability to understand the language was zero. And, as expected, I did not comprehend any of the sentences or passages as written.

This theory is widely accepted and is very helpful as educators consider our students. We have all seen students who are able to read a passage aloud with accuracy and fluency, but when you ask them to speak about what they read they sit silent. Likewise, we have students who are active contributors to high-level conversations after a read aloud but struggle to fluently decode words with more than one syllable. This model also connects to the Four-Part Processing Model, with the phonological and orthographic processing systems mostly enabling word recognition and the meaning and context processing systems covering language comprehension.

This theory is helpful to us as we plan our instruction and interventions and directs us to spend time across the various components of reading instruction. We will spend more time on the areas of reading instruction in the next chapter, but first, we will examine one more model that goes into more detail about what skills make up both factors, word recognition and language comprehension, in the Simple View of Reading.

Scarborough's Reading Rope

The last model that we will discuss was developed by Hollis Scarborough in 2001 (Figure 1.3). Scarborough is a developmental psychologist and reading researcher and developed this model to convey the specific skills within language comprehension and word recognition that are required for proficient reading. She uses the rope as a metaphor to demonstrate the way the strands come together to make skilled reading strong. Just like a rope is made stronger by the strands that come together to tightly wind into rope, skilled reading becomes stronger when these skills become automatic and strategic.

Like the Simple View of Reading, this model breaks reading down into language comprehension and word recognition. The ultimate goal of the model is for "[s]killed Reading [as a] fluent execution and coordination of word recognition and text comprehension." When this is happening, the reader is scanning over text without effort, making meaning from and connections within the text. Most words are recognized automatically, and words that need to be decoded are done so quickly and accurately. All of these components are happening at the same time, like the rope at the end, tightly woven together.

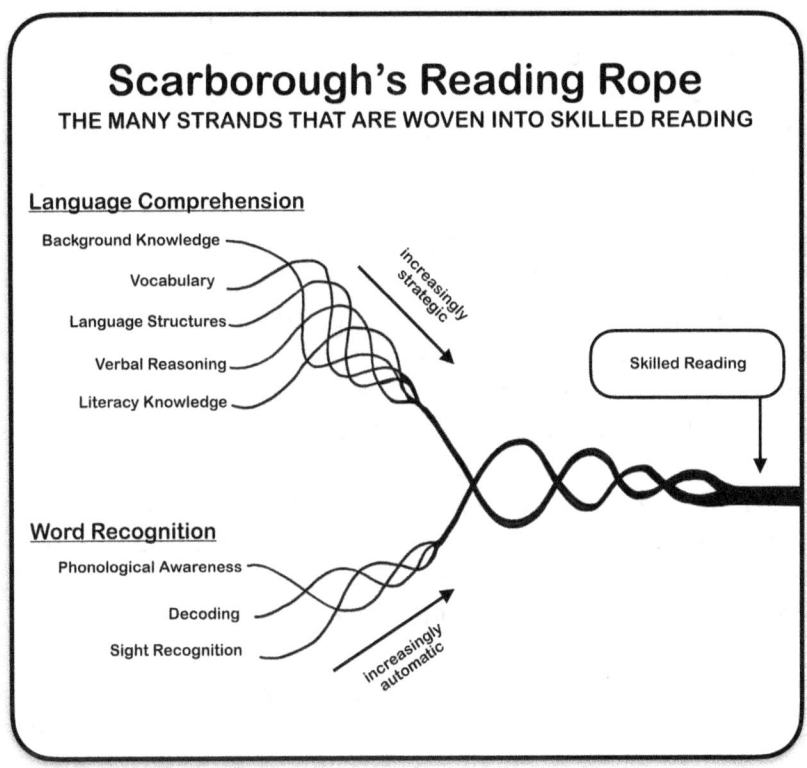

FIGURE 1.3 Scarborough's Reading Rope (Scarborough, 2001)

If you are a skilled reader, it is unlikely that you are able to identify what you are doing while you are reading. Skilled reading feels automatic, and as such, it is hard to describe the components that make it so. The specific strands provide parents and educators with an understanding of the various components that work together to build a strong reader, making it easier to prioritize monitoring and support across all skills.

Scarborough's Rope is divided up into two different strands, which weave together to create skilled reading: **language comprehension** and **word recognition**.

The language comprehension strands are **background knowledge, vocabulary, language structure, verbal reasoning, and literacy knowledge**. Background knowledge refers to a reader's familiarity with various facts and concepts. The importance of background knowledge for reading comprehension has been studied frequently. In the popular book *The Knowledge Gap*, Natalie Wexler explores in depth how the lack of content-rich curriculum in elementary schools contributes to persistent inequities in reading outcomes (2019). We know the meaning processing system works through connections of ideas and concepts, supporting the idea that the more a reader knows about a topic, the easier it will be for them to comprehend when they read about.

The word recognition strands are **phonological awareness, decoding, and sight recognition.** Phonological awareness happens in the phonological processing system, involving the identification and manipulation of phonemes, syllables, and other word parts. Decoding involves spelling sound correspondence, matching graphemes to phonemes in the brain's "letterbox." And finally, sight recognition is when, after much exposure to a particular word, the brain is able to map that string of letters as one unit to allow for instant and automatic recognition of a word.

Scarborough, in a presentation for The Reading League in 2023, emphasizes that the strands do not develop independently of one another. Instruction and mastery in one strand will also influence progress in the others. For example, the more fluently you are able to decode, the more background knowledge you may acquire by being able to access more texts. As these two strands become more automatic and strategic, readers are able to begin applying them simultaneously with increased ease.

All of this research offers educators a strong foundation for how to change our practices and teach children how to read more effectively. However, as I showed in the introduction, many early childhood educators are the product of graduate programs that may not have prioritized this information or have been required to use curricula that have not been aligned. Additionally, educators have their hands full with their daily responsibilities and aren't always able to access research published in industry journals and presented at conferences.

Fortunately, in the late 1990s, a group of researchers and practitioners came together to offer us a framework for how to align research with practice. In the next chapter, I will share that framework and use it as a way to understand how fingerplays are an evidenced-based approach aligned with the science of reading.

> **Handy Highlights**
>
> ☞ Learning to read physically changes the brain's structure, developing new pathways to process information.
> ☞ The Four-Part Processing Model is a useful way to demonstrate the complexity of mental activity happening while we read. It illustrates that reading is dependent on created pathways in the language and visual processing areas of our brain.
> ☞ The Simple View of Reading is a theory that explains how reading comprehension is the product of printed word recognition and language comprehension.
> ☞ Scarborough's Rope is another literacy model. It divides up the components of skilled reading into two different strands: language comprehension and word recognition. Both strands are comprised of essential skills that, when applied strategically and automatically, allow for skilled reading.

References

Amplify Education, Inc. (2018). Science of reading: A primer, Part 1. Amplify.

Dehaene, S. (2009). *Reading in the brain: The new science of how we read.* Penguin.

Gough, P. B., & Tunmer, W. E. (1986). Decoding, reading, and reading disability. *Remedial and Special Education, 7*(1), 6–10.

Moats, L. C. (2020). *Teaching reading is rocket science: What expert teachers of reading should know and be able to do.* American Federation of Teachers.

Moats, L. C., & Tolman, C. A. (2019). *LETRS: Language essentials for teachers of reading and spelling* (3rd ed.). Voyager Sopris Learning.

Nielsen, M. A., & Chuang, I. L. (2010). *Quantum computation and quantum information* (10th Anniversary ed.). Cambridge University Press.

Scarborough, H. S. (2001). The Scarborough reading rope: A framework for understanding the complexity of skilled reading. *Topics in Language Disorders, 21*(1), 1–23.

Seidenberg, M. S., & McClelland, J. L. (1989). A distributed, developmental model of word recognition and naming. *Psychological Review, 96*(4), 523–568.

The Reading League. (2022). Science of reading: Defining guide. https://www.thereadingleague.org/wp-content/uploads/2022/03/Science-of-Reading-eBook-2022.pdf

The Reading League. (2023). The reading rope: Key ideas behind the metaphor. https://www.thereadingleague.org/wp-content/uploads/2023/11/TRLC-Educators-and-Specialists-The-Reading-Rope-Key-Ideas-Behind-the-Metaphor.pdf

Wexler, N. (2019). *The knowledge gap: The hidden cause of America's broken education system—and how to fix it.* Avery.

Additional Readings

Climbing the Ladder of Reading & Writing: Meeting the Needs of ALL Learners edited by Nancy Young and Jan Hasbrouck

Language at the Speed of Sight: How We Read, Why So Many Can't, and What Can Be Done About It by Mark Seidenberg

Proust and the Squid: The Story and Science of the Reading Brain by Maryanne Wolf

Reading in the Brain: The New Science of How We Read by Stanislas Dehaene

Teaching Reading Is Rocket Science, 2020: What Expert Teachers of Reading Should Know and Be Able to Do by Louisa Moats

The Reading Mind: A Cognitive Approach to Understanding How the Mind Reads by Daniel T. Willingham

2

The Magic of Rhymes

In 1997, the National Institute of Child Health and Human Development (NICHD) and the Department of Education created the National Reading Panel. The National Reading Panel evaluated existing research to determine the most effective methods for teaching children to read. The panel reviewed relevant research and experiments about reading, including those summarized in Chapter 1, that met a rigorous set of standards and criteria. These findings were synthesized and the panel used them to form a set of recommendations to guide instruction and improve literacy outcomes.

The National Reading Panel's final report focused on five critical components of reading instruction (Figure 2.1):

1. **Phonemic awareness**: Understanding and manipulating phonemes in spoken words
2. **Phonics**: Systematic instruction in letter-sound relationships
3. **Fluency**: Developing the ability to read with speed, accuracy, and proper expression
4. **Vocabulary**: Teaching a wide understanding of word meanings
5. **Text comprehension**: The ability to apply comprehension strategies while reading (National Reading Panel, 2000)

These recommendations offer a concise focus for instruction while accounting for what the research tells us about how we learn to read. As this chapter shows, the use of fingerplays with instruction supports these five areas in the early childhood classroom.

The models and theories shared in Chapter 1 help us to better understand the importance of each of these five components. It is important to remember that, while these five components are distinct skills, instruction in one area often improves performance across others. As the discussed models represent, reading requires simultaneous application of many discrete skills. We will explore each of the five pillars in depth, highlighting the ways that regular use of fingerplays can support the development of the skills within it.

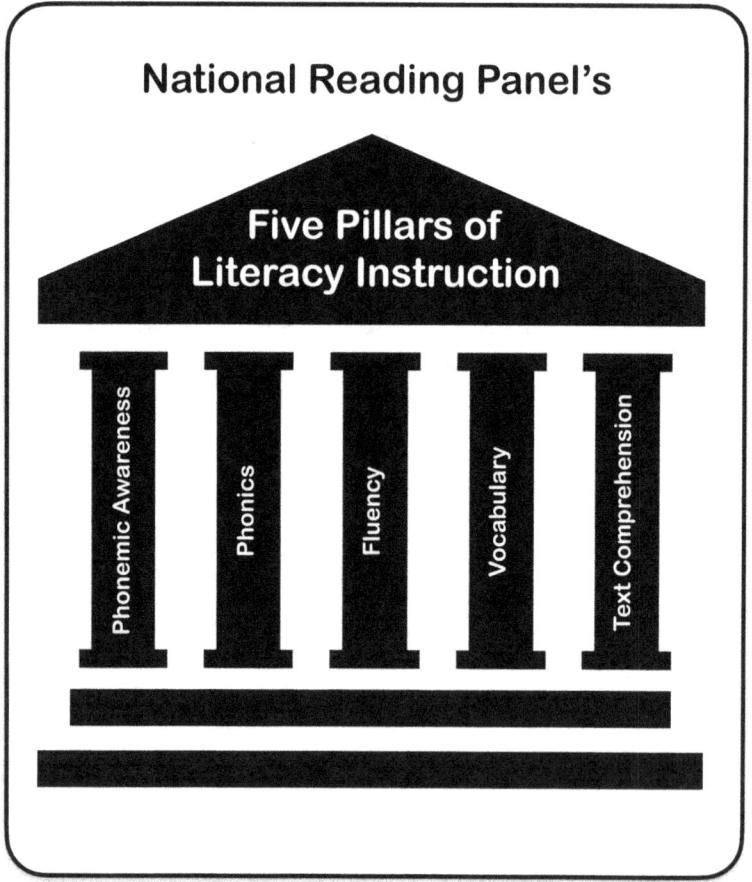

FIGURE 2.1 The Five Pillars of Literacy Instruction (National Reading Panel, 2000)

Phonemic Awareness

The first component the panel identified is **phonemic awareness,** the ability to identify, hear, and manipulate the individual phonemes within spoken words. A **phoneme** is the smallest unit of sounds in a language, such as the sound the letter "g" makes in the word "bug." Phonemic awareness includes blending and segmenting phonemes, adding phonemes, deleting phonemes, and substituting phonemes.

Phonemic awareness, focused on working with individual speech sounds, is one of the skills under the umbrella of phonological awareness. **Phonological awareness** is the ability to recognize and manipulate any of the sound structures of spoken language, not just phonemes. As shown in Figure 2.2, there

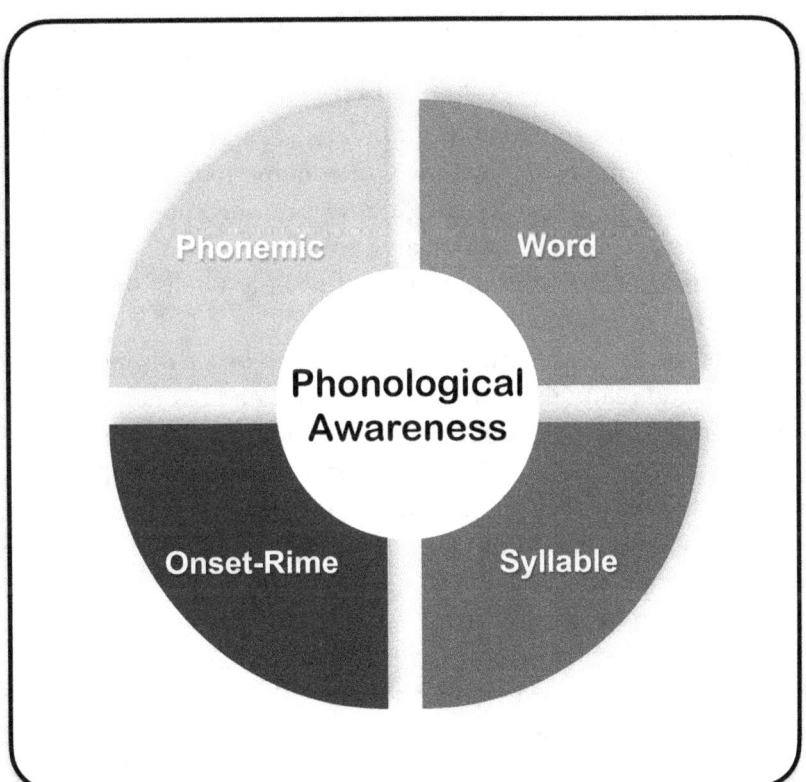

FIGURE 2.2 The Components of Phonological Awareness

are various components to phonological awareness: word awareness, syllable awareness, onset-rime awareness, and phonemic awareness. Phonemic awareness is the most complicated component of phonological awareness. While the National Reading Panel specifically mentioned phonemic awareness as a core pillar of literacy instruction, focusing instruction on all components of phonological awareness can help children become more proficient in how they hear, identify, and manipulate sounds. I'll expand this section on phonemic awareness to focus on how fingerplays are a good place to practice *all* components of phonological awareness, including phonemic awareness. Many of the strengths of using fingerplays touch on several elements of phonological awareness, not just phonemic awareness.

While we defined phonemic awareness above, let's define the other components of phonological awareness before we establish their link to fingerplays. Word awareness involves understanding the concept of a word. This is a foundational literacy skill and one that many students struggle to understand. When we learn to speak, we just speak, without awareness of how sounds bind together to form words, or how words come together to express specific ideas in sentences. Beginning to build the concept of a spoken word that contains meaning will later allow students to apply this knowledge in reading and writing where the concept of the word is essential for success.

Here's a simple example to show how word awareness helps us speak and read: my mother's sister is named Elaine, and she is always referred to as Aunt Elaine. However, when I was a child, I thought her name was Lane, and once asked my mother why she was the only aunt I had that we referred to as "Aunty." You see, Aunty Lane and Aunt Elaine sound the same! Once I learned that her name was Elaine and not Lane, I was able to properly segment the two words.

Similarly, a child who hears their parents tell them to "go to bed" every night might not understand the difference between the three words and assume that they sleep in a "gotobed."

Syllable awareness involves awareness of syllables within words and can look like counting, segmenting, adding, or deleting syllables. Being proficient in these syllable skills orally and audibly prepares students for spelling and reading multisyllabic words. For example, if you want to spell the word "basketball," you would first need to segment the word into syllables, and from there segment each sound in each syllable (bas/ket/ball) to match the sounds to letters.

Onset-rime awareness breaks down syllables into the onset (the initial consonant or consonant blend that comes before the vowel) and the rime (the part of the syllable that includes the vowel and the sounds that follow it). In the word "cat," the onset is "/c/" and the rime is "/at/." In the word play, the onset is "/pl/" and the rime is "/ay/."

Fingerplays are a fertile place for students to practice all components of phonological awareness. When rehearsing a fingerplay with students, you are helping to establish the concept of a word every time you pause to allow them to fill in a "blank," or when you repeat a rhyme again and again, omitting a word each time. Helping them to recognize that our speech is not a continuous flow of sounds, but instead words that come together to build discrete meaningful phrases and sentences, is providing them with a foundation to understand how we use an established language, full of words, to convey information. This foundation of understanding of our shared language will allow them to learn other skills – like reading.

Rhyming is another component of word awareness, as it considers a word as a whole and works to produce and compare other words in relation to it. It is a common focus for phonological awareness activities in early childhood education. There are different levels of difficulty within rhyming tasks. First, children are taught what a rhyme is – words that share the same ending sounds. Then they work to recognize when a pair of words rhymes or not. After they are able to recognize a rhyme spoken orally, the next step would be producing a rhyming word. For example, "who can give me a word that rhymes with chair?"

Action rhymes like fingerplays are often children's first exposure to rhyming words. Almost all hinge on the incorporation of rhyming words, and in some cases, you can use them as opportunities to have students come up with rhymes on their own.

My son and I were participating in a Music Together class in the spring of 2020. When COVID stay-at-home orders were established, our incredibly talented music instructor did what so many of us did that year and took to Zoom. I remember smiling at the computer during one session when she began to sing one of my favorite fingerplays:

Two Little Birds

Two little birds sitting on a hill
One named Jack and one named Jill
Fly away Jack, Fly away Jill
Come back Jack, Come back Jill

However, where I usually stop, she kept going. Much to the delight of my almost three-year-old, she continued:

Two little birds, sitting on a cloud
One named quiet, one name LOUD *(saying the name of "LOUD" - you guessed it - quite loud, to squeals of laughter from my son)*
Fly away quiet, fly away LOUD
Come back quiet, come back LOUD.

She finished this verse and I saw the boxes on the Zoom screen filled with smiling children. Next she asked, "What else could we call these two birds? Who can think of two opposite ideas?" The speakers were loud with suggestions: hot and cold! Wet and dry! Short and tall!

She continued: "If we name them short and tall, where would they have to be sitting? Who can think of a place that rhymes with tall?"

Soon we were all singing,

Two little birds, sitting on a wall
One named Short and one named Tall
Fly away Short, fly away Tall
Come back Short, come back Tall!

She so beautifully modeled how you can use shared rhymes as a way to play with language. And what is "identifying, hearing and manipulating" sounds, as required in mastering phonological awareness, if not playing with them? Whenever you have shared language, as we do when we use fingerplays, you have an opportunity to build, innovate, and play with the sounds within.

As you continue to use rhymes with the children in your life, you are helping them to build their own collection of our shared language. Besides modifying the words and sentence composition, you can also begin to play with individual sounds within words. Segmenting and blending individual sounds, an essential component of phonemic awareness, is what allows us to go from reading a sound at a time to blending sounds together to read words. When a student is sounding out the word "frog," they will start by naming the individual sounds "/f/, /r/, /o/, /g/." Unless they can then blend those sounds together, they will not be able to successfully read that word.

However, before students can segment and blend sounds, they will begin with identifying the first sound they hear in a word. You can challenge students to repeat a short rhyme, but instead of completing it in the traditional way, encourage them to change the rhyme so every word begins with the same sound. Instead of "Itsy Bitsy Spider," you may be singing the "Witsy, Witsy, Wider." Think of the traditional "name game" when "Meghan" seamlessly takes on the beginning sounds of "bo" (Beghan) and "fo" (Feghan). Playing with language in this way helps to prepare the brain for the phoneme-level work required of readers once they adequately map the relationship between printed letters and speech sounds.

Using fingerplays that play with rhymes, even as simple as the name game, will introduce the idea of segmenting, adding, changing, or deleting sounds to children without them knowing it, helping to start them on their path toward reading.

Phonics

The next critical component from the National Reading Panel is something that has gotten the most attention as more people are becoming familiar with the science of reading: phonics. Phonics instruction is focused on the relationship between printed letters, or **graphemes**, and the sounds they represent, or **phonemes** (as discussed in the previous section). Phonics instruction helps to build the brain's "letterbox," as described by Stanislas Dehaene and covered in the previous chapter. Essentially, teaching phonics helps readers to decode words.

The research is clear – all readers use phonics or "letter/sound" connections to figure out known and unknown words. This knowledge replaced the previously accepted "Three Cueing" theory, which proposed that readers use a combination of phonics, sentence structure, and context to figure out a word. Now that we know reading hinges on fluent recall of these letter/sound relationships, the systematic teaching of phonics must be an essential part of reading instruction. Since fingerplays are largely done without print, phonics may not seem like a natural point of connection; however, once we dig into the various concepts that make up phonics, it is clear that intentional use of fingerplays can help further skill development in this area as well.

Phonics instruction includes a few essential components. The first is the alphabetic principle, which is the understanding that letters represent sounds. This concept is crucial for children's ability to begin forming the connection between graphemes and phonemes. As adults, it seems obvious that print carries meaning, but this crucial understanding is an important step toward developing decoding skills.

Every time an adult reads something, they are modeling the alphabetic principle for children. While fingerplays are often done orally, there are a number of picture books that are full of printed versions. These books are great resources for learning rhymes, but also for sharing them with children. While you can certainly introduce fingerplays orally and with an anchoring image, as I describe in Chapter 5, when you read a rhyme from a book or share a printed version to go home, children are learning that the rhyme they have come to love can be represented by a series of letters and letter combinations.

Another component of phonics is decoding. Decoding is the process of "sounding out words," or identifying the word's phonemes and blending them together. For example, reading the word "map" out loud requires seeing the letters "m," "a," and "p," and then identifying the associated sounds of /m/, /a/, and /p/. Then, one must blend those sounds together to produce the spoken word "map." This requires the blending and segmenting discussed in the previous section on phonemic awareness, but also a fluent connection between the spoken sound and written letter.

Encoding is another component of phonics that is the process of spelling words by segmenting their sounds and matching the sounds to their corresponding letters. When you want to spell the word "chip" you may slowly recite each sound, /ch/, /i/, /p/, and write the letter or letters that represent this sound. Encoding also includes learning letter formation or how to write the letter.

While they are not traditional fingerplays, many educators use rhymes to help students learn correct letter formation. For example:

Straight line down
Then across, across
You made an F just like a boss!

Many educators also use chants with corresponding hand motions to help students build associations between letters and sounds. For example:

A apple /a/ – /a/, /a/, /a/ (point up like to an apple in a tree)
B bat /b/ - /b/, /b/, /b/ (swing a bat)
C cat /c/ - /c/, /c/, /c/ (use three fingers on each hand to make whiskers on your face)

While fingerplays will certainly not be the main way of teaching phonics, the idea of using rhyme and movement together while teaching letter names and sounds certainly helps students master this essential skill.

Fluency

Once students are able to decode words, we hope to see them reading with fluency, the next critical component from the National Reading Panel. **Fluency** is the ability to read words with speed, accuracy, and proper expression. This involves reading in phrases, or groups of words that make sense together. It also involves changing the intonation of your voice to reflect what is happening in the sentence.

Being able to read with speed and accuracy depends on the letter and sound connections made in the brain. As demonstrated in the models examined in chapter one, readers are storing letters and strands of letters as connections to sounds. As these connections strengthen, recall becomes easier and quicker. So much of this work happens through phonics and phonemic awareness instruction and practice, as discussed in the previous two sections. However, when we look for reading fluency, we must also account for reading with proper pacing, expression, intonation (including pitch, tone, volume), and emphasis on certain words. If someone accuses you of stealing their parking spot, and you know you carefully chose an unassigned spot in the lot this morning, you may reply, "I most certainly did *not*," changing your voice to emphasize "not." This is known as **prosody**, the rhythmic and melodic elements of speech.

Fingerplays offer an excellent place to practice prosody. The rhymes are designed to be recited with rhythm, emphasizing certain words by playing with pacing or intonation. Consider the following rhyme.

The Little Turtle

There was a little turtle, who lived in a box (put one hand over the other and circle the thumbs)
He swam in a puddle (make swimming motions)
He climbed on the rocks (use your fingers to climb up your arm)
He **snapped** at a mosquito (clap hands)
He **snapped** at a flea (clap hands)
He **snapped** at a minnow (clap hands)
He **snapped** at me(clap hands)
He *caught* the mosquito (grab with your hand)
He *caught* the flea (grab with your hand)
He *caught* the minnow (grab with your hand)
But he didn't catch me (shake finger)

This rhyme has a steady, rhythmic flow due to its regular meter and repetition of phrases. In this rhyme, we change our voice to reflect the nature of what is happening. For example, when saying "snapped," our voice may get louder and sharper. Before we begin the section on what the turtle caught, we will pause to show a change in subject, and our voice may soften as we say the word "caught." Finally, when we say "but he didn't catch me," we use a sing-song voice to sound like we are teasing the turtle.

What makes these rhymes engaging is the rhythm and prosody we recite them with. In the example from my son's music class during COVID, when reciting "quiet," we all brought the volume of our voice down, and when reciting "loud," we were loud!

To help teach physical self-regulation, you can prompt students to recite the rhymes at different speeds and volumes. A beloved kindergarten teacher I worked with would pretend to turn a dial, asking students to speed up or slow down as they completed a rhyme or song. Sometimes I challenge my students to complete a fingerplay without making any noise, reciting the words in their head as they complete their hand motions. All of these suggestions for how to use fingerplays help to build the foundation for reading fluency, especially if you draw attention to what you are doing and even name it with the language we will use when discussing reading fluency.

Once students have developed sufficient decoding skills, they can practice reading established fingerplays. Because they have a sense of the rhythm of the language from practicing orally, they will be able to practice reading while changing the pacing, expression, and intonation of the words they are reading. The understanding of the spoken fingerplay helps the student practice the components of fluency in reading. In Chapter 5, I suggest ways to send printed rhymes home with children to facilitate this practice.

Fluency is often referred to as the bridge between decoding and reading comprehension. When students are able to read text without effort, with proper phrasing and prosody, it is more likely that they will understand what they are reading. While this relies on rapid recollection of orthographic connections, the oral work we do with language while reciting fingerplays exposes children to the ways you can change your speech to emphasize certain sounds and impact meaning.

Comprehension and Content Knowledge

When we read a text, we read it in the context of everything we already know about reading as well as the content of the text, which is why comprehension and content knowledge was listed as another pillar by the National Reading Panel. For example, when we read a book about a family, we use our preexisting knowledge about families and what we know about them to make sense of what we read. This is true for more complex informational topics as well, like animal defense mechanisms and the workings of our solar system.

When students have more information about a topic, it helps them access what they are reading. Activating appropriate background knowledge before reading a new text is a common teaching method to help support reading comprehension.

I'll share a passage from the previous chapter to illustrate what I mean:

> *Suppose we have two quits. If these were two classical bits, then there would be four possible states, 00, 01, 10, and 11.*

Early readers may not be able to read this sentence out loud, but by the time they leave elementary school, most students will be able to. However, I would also imagine few of them would *comprehend* what this sentence meant. I would imagine very few of the people reading this book can comprehend what this sentence means, given that it is referring to complex quantum physics concepts. Without the appropriate content knowledge, there is no way to understand – and truly read – this sentence.

While perhaps not the *most* impactful way to build and activate content knowledge, using fingerplays and rhymes that connect to the content you are teaching and learning can be a helpful tool. Students frequently build knowledge through reading informational text, intentional use of video and audio clips, or listening to experts. But content fingerplays can make the learning of content knowledge more fun for students and can reinforce or supplement whatever other instruction on content you have throughout your day.

Leo Lionni's book *Fish is Fish* is one of my favorites to read with young children. In addition to being an engaging story with a great message about being yourself, it exposes children to the concept of metamorphosis and animal classifications. Imagine a lesson where you are teaching children about the life cycle of a frog, and you plan to read *Fish is Fish*. You can begin your lesson, to center the children's attention, like this:

Tadpole

Tadpole, tadpole, swimming in a pail (hands together moving back and forth)
Big round head and a wiggly tail (point to your head and then shake your hips)
Someday soon four legs will sprout (hold up four fingers)
Then you will be a frog and hop right out! (hop up and down on the last three words)

By using this fingerplay, you are priming your students for the lesson by giving a bit of content knowledge to supplement the book you are about to read. It also offers them a helpful rhyme to remember what happens through the life cycle of a frog – similar to how fingerplays can help children remember how to write letters, as described in the section on phonics.

Many early childhood classrooms also teach students about the lifecycle of a butterfly, often bringing in caterpillars for students to observe. Beginning each lesson or observation with the following rhyme will help students remember content words and concepts necessary for describing what they are witnessing.

Caterpillars

"Let's go to sleep" the caterpillar said (place palms together under side of head)
As it tucked itself into its chrysalis beds. (make a fist and wrap the other hand around it)
It will awaken by and by (slowly unfold and hold up fingers)
And slowly emerge as a butterfly (link thumbs and hands make flying motion)

These examples are just a start! There are countless incredible fingerplays in existence, and they are easy to create on your own. From gardening to community helpers, family members, or American symbols, using fingerplays helps build content and understanding, while making your thematic study live throughout the day in your classroom.

Vocabulary

Vocabulary is the last component of literacy instruction recommended by the National Reading Panel. Like content knowledge, having a wide vocabulary allows students to make meaning from the words they are reading. Vocabulary instruction should be systematic, explicit, and embedded in meaningful reading and language activities. As this pillar relates to fingerplays, the implications are similar as to the previous section on comprehension and content knowledge. Fingerplays can be an effective – and fun – way to introduce new words to students.

Many students enter school lacking in vocabulary, from basic words that are used in everyday conversation to more academic terms or content-specific vocabulary. In the past, I have taught a unit about sound and how it is caused by vibration. All of the students in our class struggle to remember, never mind appropriately use, the word vibration.

Ideally, vocabulary instruction will include a focus on morphemic awareness. A **morpheme** is a unit of meaning, such as a root, suffix, or prefix. A morpheme may not be a word on its own, but it does come with meaning. For example, the suffix "tion" means, "the act of." When learning the word "vibration," students can learn that vibrate means "to move quickly back and forth," and that -tion means "the act of," making vibration mean "the act of moving quickly back and forth." The more work students do with morphemic awareness, the better suited they will be to figure out new words using morphemes they have previously encountered.

Teaching a fingerplay that we repeat before our science lesson, in addition to teaching the word explicitly as a part of the lesson and using it in our work, has helped their comfort with the word and their ability to retain its meaning and even use it correctly in speech.

This is the fingerplay:

Vibrations

Every sound that you can hear (tap your ears with each hand)
Is from vibrations, that is clear (shake both hands quickly)
Touch your throat and feel them go (touch your throat)
Vibrations moving to and fro
(making a humming noise) - students will feel the vibration

New vocabulary words need to be used frequently if we want students to remember them and eventually add them to their mental dictionaries. By incorporating vocabulary words into our fingerplays, we will increase how often they are used and help deepen their meaning for students. The greater their vocabulary, the more they will be able to access new information in reading.

The National Reading Panel gave us a helpful framework for thinking about evidence-based approach to literacy instruction. Each of the five pillars are important components to help kids learn how to read, and the use of fingerplays can support each of them. I am not suggesting that fingerplays, on their own, help children learn to read, but they can be a fun and engaging way to support the other aspects of your curriculum. I have included a list of additional texts at the end of this chapter that go more in depth about each of the five pillars if you are interested in learning more.

Fingerplays have many other benefits beyond literacy instruction. Their regular use can support the growth and development of the whole child, which I will cover in the next chapter.

> **Handy Highlights**
>
> ☞ The National Reading Panel used reading science and research to determine the most effective methods for teaching children to read. The panel used these findings to form a set of recommendations to guide instruction and improve literacy outcomes.
> ☞ The National Reading Panel created "five pillars" for literacy instruction: phonemic awareness, phonics, fluency, comprehension and content knowledge, and vocabulary.
> ☞ Fingerplays can augment and support literacy instruction in each of these five evidence-based pillars.

Reference

National Reading Panel. (2000). *Teaching children to read: An evidence-based assessment of the scientific research literature on reading and its implications for reading instruction.* National Institute of Child Health and Human Development.

Additional Readings

Equipped for Reading Success: A Comprehensive, Step-By-Step Program for Developing Phonemic Awareness and Fluent Word Recognition by David A. Kilpatrick

Reading Fluency: Understand, Assess, Teach by Jan Hasbrouck and Deborah Glaser

Speech to Print: Language Essentials for Teachers by Louisa Moats

The Reading Comprehension Blueprint: Helping Students Make Meaning from Text by Nancy Lewis Hennessy

Understanding and Teaching Reading Comprehension: A Handbook by Carsten Elbro, Jane Oakhill, and Kate Cain

3

Beyond Literacy

As early childhood educators, our students come to us at the beginning stages of their development. While we have seen the objectives of the early childhood classroom become more and more academic, the physical and emotional development of our students has not changed. Unfortunately, sometimes the increased academic demands can come at the expense of time and focus on the important social, emotional, and physiological development of students. Despite the increased demands, we should not lose focus on the underlying physical and emotional skills that are required in order for our students to access, and more importantly, enjoy school in today's world.

When I was originally revisiting the use of fingerplays in my classroom I was pleased to discover that their use supported what we know about how students learn how to read, and the science behind that process. However, after expanding my research, I was also able to clearly see the connection between using fingerplays and the development of other important foundational skills. In this section, I will provide an overview of other skills our students need to access and enjoy school and how the regular use of fingerplays can benefit children in these areas. This chapter will touch on social development, students' fine and gross motor development, as well as their self-regulation skills. Finally, I will discuss the benefits of using fingerplays to promote speech and language development.

Social Benefits

School, like any gathering of people, is ripe for social learning. Children spend the bulk of their waking hours at school interacting with peers and teachers. Schools, while certainly responsible for teaching academic content and skills, must also tackle teaching character development and social skills, both directly and indirectly. Spend an hour in a kindergarten classroom and you will observe that, in the midst of teaching letter sounds, the adults in the room are teaching emotional regulation, mediating peer conflict, and maybe even how to put on a jacket independently. Additionally, children are constantly learning from their peers. Behaviors are observed and tried on for size, knowledge is passed around, and friendships are formed, strengthened, and changed every day. I remember being shocked when my son, who had never heard of Pokémon before beginning first grade, came home able to list "health" statistics about specific Pokémon he could identify with ease. Because of this, we know children are developing their sense of self and their understanding of community at school. Is it possible that participating in shared fingerplays can have a role in building this sense of community and social-emotional intelligence?

In his book *The Anxious Generation* Jonathan Haidt writes a chapter titled "What Children Need to Do in Childhood." While this chapter covers a variety of behaviors, he spends time discussing the importance of attunement. Attunement refers to a natural adjusting and synchronizing of movements and emotions with other humans. As babies, this looks like mimicking facial expressions and responding to silly adults with coos and giggles. As children develop into toddlers and develop speech, attunement expands, including learning how to engage in verbal back and forth in conversation and reading facial expressions. Haidt (2024) highlights the importance of attunement as children age:

> As children get older, they go beyond turn taking to find joy in perfect synchrony, doing the same thing at the same time as their partner. Girls especially come to delight in

singing songs together, jumping rope together, or playing rhyming and clapping games (such as pat-a-cake) in which high-speed hand motions are perfectly matched between the partners while high-speed nonsense songs are sung at the same time. Such games have no explicit goal or way to win. They are pleasurable because they use the ancient power of synchrony to create communion between unrelated people. (p.57).

From here, Hadith summarizes research about collective rituals, including rhymes but also bigger synchronous movements happening alongside music. He shares how expansive this tradition is, spanning every continent and happening for generations and generations. He cites an experiment that shows how synchronous movement can help to foster a sense of fellowship and belonging, something anyone who has sang along with "New York, New York," at the end of a winning Yankees game (or "Sweet Caroline" if you're a Red Sox fan), can attest to.

In a world that has moved more and more toward asynchronous connection (text messages, recorded videos, etc.), the need for attunement has become even more pronounced. Whenever I start a fingerplay with a group of students, I feel like I can reset the group and their behavior. Perhaps I was attempting to get through a lesson quickly and got frustrated when students were disengaged or distracted. Maybe there was a conflict between two children competing for a favorite spot on the carpet. Possibly I was dealing with a child who had a bloody nose and the draw of silliness with friends took over in the meantime.

There are countless ways that we, as a collective group of children and the adults who guide them, separate from one another. And while that is natural and fine, there is beauty in bringing us back together. Beginning a fingerplay and watching as all the small mouths and hands perform a well-rehearsed and loved rhyme in sync is a true example of communion, not unlike in a house of worship. And while we are often reciting silly rhymes instead of ancient hymns, the important piece is that we are doing it together. This uniting ritual brings us together, literally, and I believe it can have an impact beyond the 30 seconds it takes to recite "Open and Shut Them."

If Haidt is describing a break from communion with each other, and the inability to socially learn from other humans as a result of increased screen time and asynchronous communication, fingerplays can bring back that communion in one small way into our classroom. It's not the only thing we need to strengthen our socio-emotional learning in the classroom – Haidt offers many different recommendations in his book – but it's an easily adopted and quickly understood intervention that we can bring to our daily practice.

Fine and Gross Motor

In the introduction, I described the magic that I felt when I first started using fingerplays in my classroom. There have been other, non-rhyme-related moments when that magic settled over myself and my students. A few weeks into my first year teaching, I was overwhelmed with the weight of teaching 22 four-year-olds. I was spending all my time planning lessons, researching the best way to engage my students, and preparing materials to give them hands-on learning opportunities. One evening, after staying late at school to cut out who knows how many pages of laminated materials, I stopped at the local grocery store to buy myself something to eat for dinner. This was not my regular grocery store, so there was a lot of aisle-wandering happening as I tried to figure out what I wanted. At one point, I found myself in the "seasonal" aisle, which was full of an incredibly random assortment of things. As I moved quickly through, eager to find something easy to prepare for dinner, something in the "clearance" section caught my eye. There were a few boxes of play doh, marked 50% off. I threw two of the boxes filled with those instantly recognizable yellow cylinders into my cart without thinking too much about it and then moved on to the frozen meal section.

When I parked at my school the next morning, the play doh boxes were still sitting in my passenger seat. I grabbed them on my way and quickly placed an opened can at each of the tiny student chairs on my tables. Without any instruction, my students entered 40 minutes later, hung their coats and backpacks, and literally dug in. It was the first morning that I was able to greet each of my students and welcome them into a calm and engaged classroom. Every single student was thrilled to see the play doh waiting at their spot and began squishing, rolling, pinching, and creating immediately. This "play doh" morning was another moment of magic, where not only were my students quiet and calm, they were actively working their imaginations alongside the many small muscles in their hands and arms.

Like the play doh on my students' chairs, the movement of fingerplays can also offer students a chance to experience and discover their own fine motor and gross motor skills. Fingerplays do this not in a structured manner, but through play (it's in the name, after all). They allow the students to discover their fingers, hands, and arms all on their own, in a structured way with repeated direction from the instructor.

Fine Motor

Fine motor work refers to the small, accurate movements made by our hands and fingers. While the movements we make with our feet and toes are also examples of fine motor, our work in the classroom is usually not focused there. Fine motor control is a complex progress that incorporates a variety of skills including coordination, muscle strength, dexterity, and awareness and planning. Fine motor skills are required for many components of life, both in and out of the classroom. Some examples of fine motor skills include fastening shoe straps, buttons, or tying laces. Fine motor skills also include twisting a doorknob, picking up an object with your fingers, and eating using a fork or a spoon. In school, we depend on fine motor skills for a variety of activities such as holding a pencil, marker, or crayon and writing or drawing with it. We also ask students to use scissors to cut or to take the top off of a glue stick to paste something together.

As early childhood educators, we may be familiar with the fine motor milestones that mark typical development. These milestones begin with things like grasping and transferring as a baby, and move to stacking blocks and self-feeding in the toddler years. As students get closer to preschool age, these milestones include things like turning the pages of books and holding utensils with their fingers, and eventually drawing copies of certain shapes and using their nondominant (or "helper" hand) to help them stabilize objects. By kindergarten, we expect students to be able to cut out shapes, color in a controlled manner, and use a three-fingered grasp on writing utensils while demonstrating proper number and letter formation.

When I introduced the play doh to my students, it was instantly engaging and felt like classroom magic. When we look at all of the components of fine motor development, it is clear that playing with play doh or putty is also purposeful work, a winning combination in my (and this) book. And while my love for play doh runs deep, it is not a tool that can easily be pulled out at a moment's notice without mess, management, and potential squabbles over color preference and air hardened dough. Enter (once again): the fingerplay.

What distinguishes a fingerplay from a nursery rhyme or a song is the use of… well, fingers! For each of the rhymes included in this collection, and in the hundreds you can find in other sources or make up on your own, there are a set of movements that go along with the words. While the movements do provide engagement and explanation of the rhyme, they are also allowing for children to practice using their fine motor skills. The term bilateral coordination refers to using both sides of the body together in one movement. Fingerplays offer children the opportunity to use both hands at the same time to act out the rhyme. Many of the actions also include manipulating the hands and fingers in specific ways, such as holding up certain fingers, pinching thumb and forefinger together, or moving hands up and down or across the midline. All of these movements engage the many muscles in the hands and fingers, while requiring students to coordinate their movements.

Let's take a look at a fingerplay from the last chapter and analyze it for the different types of fine motor work happening.

Two Little Birds

Two little blackbirds sitting on a hill (hold up one finger on each hand)
One named Jack and one named Jill (make fingers come together and touch thumb, making a beak. Open and close one at a time when saying name)
Fly away Jack, fly away Jill (fly the hands behind your back, one at a time)
Come back Jack, come back Jill (bring back the fingers, one at a time)

In this popular rhyme, we are using our fingers to illustrate what is being spoken. However, we are also using a number of fine motor skills. First, any movement requires motor planning. Motor planning is the process of figuring out how to move your body in a specific, planned way. Next, the use of both hands at the same time requires bilateral coordination. Holding one finger up at a time requires finger isolation, as opposed to the less mature movement of, say, a baby where all fingers move at the same time. When you bring the fingers together to touch down to the thumb, you are practicing opposition, where the tip of the thumb touches the tip of another finger. When strength is used in opposition, it allows for the proper use of the pincer grasp in securely holding small items.

While I know fingerplays cannot be the only way we challenge and grow our children's fine motor development, that is pretty amazing for a simple 30-second rhyme. If you are able to integrate fingerplays into numerous parts of your day with children, you will be providing them with countless ways to joyfully practice all the small and intentional movements that make up effective fine motor work.

Gross Motor

As fine motor movements are the small and accurate movements made by small muscles, gross motor movements refer to the movements of larger muscles in the arms, legs, and torso. Gross motor movements affect posture and core stability, which, in turn, can actually affect the development of fine motor strength. For example, if a child is lacking core strength and proper postural structure, it will be harder for them to use the smaller muscles required for fine motor work.

Gross motor skills involve using the whole body at once, such as required by running, jumping, and climbing. They are also required for body coordination like when walking up and down stairs, sitting with stable trunk control, hopping on one foot, and moving from lying to sitting to standing. Children are naturally very interested in engaging in gross motor movement, as evidenced by any adult attempting to move efficiently to any location with a child in tow. If there is a large rock to jump off of, they will find it. A curb to balance on, all over it. This natural inclination toward gross motor movement makes sense, as young children are constantly progressing through important gross motor milestones.

As the academic expectations for young children have advanced in the last decade, it has become more common to observe children sitting for longer periods of time throughout their day. Teachers are given sky-high expectations for what they need to accomplish throughout the year and spend as much time as possible preparing children for these academic goals. However, our children's timeline for physical development has not changed, and many students struggle with the physical and mental demands of so much direct instruction and academic work time. Children still need to use their larger muscles, and if the time is not made by the teachers for this, the students will make it happen with wiggles, lying on the carpet, rocking on chairs, and other less desirable behaviors.

While outdoor play and physical education classes can offer opportunities for gross motor movement, it is clear that teachers and caregivers need to find ways to incorporate it throughout the day. While called "fingerplays," the action rhymes we have been learning about in this book can involve muscles beyond the fingers. In fact, many of these finger rhymes demand the use of many gross motor skills that our children are developing. Let's look at a classic example.

Teddy Bear

Teddy bear, teddy bear turn around (turn in a circle)
Teddy bear, teddy bear touch the ground (bend down to touch the ground)
Teddy bear, teddy bear jump up high (jump up off of two feet)
Teddy bear, teddy bear touch the sky (stretch high)
Teddy bear, teddy bear turn and twist (twist at the hips)
Teddy bear, teddy bear blow a kiss (blow a kiss)
Teddy bear, teddy bear turn out the light (mime turning off the light)
Teddy bear, teddy bear say goodnight! (put hands together under one side of head/lay down if room)

In this rhyme, we see students moving their large muscles in many ways. They turn their whole body around in a circle but also twist at their trunk. They move up and down touching the ground and then using their whole body to jump off of two feet. They can transition from sitting to standing to begin the rhyme, and – if space allows – end up on the ground in a lying position. As with fine motor, using action rhymes alone is not enough to develop gross motor muscles, but having these opportunities sprinkled throughout the day certainly helps.

Speech and Language Development

We spent a great deal of time earlier in this book discussing how our brain uses language pathways to learn how to read. We established that we are naturally wired to learn how to speak and communicate but require instruction to learn how to read. Because of this, the chapters focused on literacy acquisition have already established the connection between using fingerplays and speech and language development. However, just as with fine and gross motor development, a child's speech and language development follows a typical path of growth, and it is worth spending some time looking at those milestones and considering the role of fingerplays when intervention is required.

With the first three years of a child's life marking the most intensive period of acquiring speech and language skills, we see children develop skills that are related to both sound understanding and production as well as communication. While speech and language are often referred to together, it is worth exploring what each term includes.

Speech refers to the specific sounds produced when making words. This includes articulation, voice, and fluency. Articulation is the actual production of sounds using our mouths, lips, and tongues. Proper articulation allows us to be understood. There are different intelligibility milestones, varying based on who is attempting to understand (a family member or a stranger) and whether or not the words are spoken in isolation or in a sentence. Speech sound development follows a typical pattern, with certain sounds developing earlier than others. Table 3.1 shows the ages that most English-speaking children develop specific sounds, according to The American Speech-Language-Hearing Association.

Voice, another component of speech, refers to the literal vibration of vocal folds in the larynx and breath, and how they produce sound. This includes the volume and pitch we produce as well as our intonation. And finally, fluency refers to the rhythm of our speech. Some people who repeat specific sounds

TABLE 3.1 Communication Milestones from Birth to Age 4

By 3 months	Makes cooing sounds
By 5 months	Laughs and makes playful sounds
By 6 months	Makes speech-like babbling sounds like **puh, ba, mi, da**
By 1 year	Babbles longer strings of sounds like **mimi, upup, bababa**
By 3 years	Says **m, n, h, w, p, b, t, d, k, g,** and **f** in words
	Familiar people understand the child's speech
By 4 years	Says **y** and **v** in words
	May still make mistakes on the **s, sh, ch, j, ng, th, z, l, and r sounds**
	Most people understand the child's speech

Source: American Speech-Language-Hearing Association (ASHA) (n.d.a, n.d.b)

or pause frequently may struggle with fluency, sometimes being diagnosed with a stutter.

Language includes both expressive and receptive language. Expressive language is the ability to communicate your thoughts, needs, and wants through verbal or nonverbal communication. Receptive language refers to understanding what others are trying to communicate.

Well-child pediatric visits provide families with information on speech and language milestones, encouraging families to pursue additional evaluation if certain milestones are unmet. A child may qualify as having either a speech sound disorder (when they fail to produce appropriate speech sounds according to developmentally appropriate guidelines) or a language disorder (where they are unable to adequately make meaning from the speech of others, or meaningfully express their own thoughts, feelings, or needs).

The earlier chapters focus on the way fingerplays can support students' speech sound production and reception, as well as the development of vocabulary and practice with fluency. Fingerplays can also help in the development of those children who need support in specific sound production and/or varying their voice tone or volume. Teachers, family members, or speech and language pathologists can prompt students to repeat rhymes that focus on particularly challenging sounds or challenge them to repeat rhymes at different volumes. Students can use rhymes to practice different pitches, or even use different breath patterns. As in other areas, fingerplays offer a foundation on which practitioners can build opportunities for specific skill rehearsal and mastery.

Self-Regulation

After my first year of teaching, my district signed up to pilot a new curriculum, called "Tools of the Mind," that claimed to teach students self-regulation skills. This was in 2011 and self-regulation was "the next big thing." Two pioneering texts drove this interest in the subject: Daniel J. Siegel and Tina Payne Bryson published

The Whole-Brain Child in 2012 and Paul Tough's book *How Children Succeed* came out in 2012. *The Whole-Brain Child* uses brain science to explain how to teach children to integrate their emotional and logical brain processes with the goal of self-regulation. *How Children Succeed* argues that skills like perseverance, curiosity, and, yes, self-control are more beneficial in lifelong success than traditionally measured "intelligence." Both of these books had an immense impact on how parents and educators considered childhood development, both emphasizing the essentialness of teaching and developing self-regulation skills in all children.

In August of 2011, I was welcoming students into my Washington, DC, kindergarten classroom. I was teaching in a Title 1 school in Southeast, DC, and was newly trained in the first months of Tools of the Mind. Tools of the Mind is an early childhood education curriculum designed with a focus on fostering self-regulation and executive functioning in early childhood. The curriculum was developed by Dr. Elena Bodrova and Dr. Deborah J. Leong (2024), and is based on the theories of developmental psychologist Lev Vygotsky.

I remember walking into our first day of Tools training, a few days before school started, having done my research. I learned about how Tools could help my students develop this important executive functioning skill and was fully invested in the importance of self-regulation. That said, I had no idea how to do it.

I ate up everything the trainers presented to us that day. The curriculum is designed to teach self-regulation, not as a subject or content like math or foundational literacy skills, but through the routines, procedures, and structures of the classroom. Each and every activity is designed to promote self-regulation through the use of partnered work, mediators that remind students of the expected rules, and the opportunity to self-check their work for accuracy. The curriculum recognizes that self-regulation is a combination of physical, cognitive, and emotional self-regulation and acknowledges that they do not all develop at the same rate. Children learn to regulate their physical behaviors first, then their emotional ones.

The curriculum also uses dramatic play as a way to practice self-regulation, helping students identify the "rules" that go along with certain situations and regulate in order to comply. For example, if acting out "The Three Billy Goats Gruff," the first Billy Goat would need to not throw the troll into the river, but somehow cleverly trick him to wait for the bigger brother. If the student acting out the story did not comply with the story and decided instead to "throw" the troll off the bridge, the other students would not be able to play their roles.

That day we learned about the theory and philosophy behind the program, and – given that we were two days away from welcoming our students – a lot about the nuts and bolts of implementation. We were given a crash course in structures like "buddy reading," which required students to take turns being the "ears" and "mouth," reading and listening to their buddies in turn. We were given a CD with a "Freeze Dance" song on it, and encouraged to teach students how to play, not only freezing when the music said to, but by mimicking a stick figure posing in a specific way that teachers would hold up when the music stopped. All of these activities were focused on physical self-regulation, investing in that as a foundational skill for all future regulation development.

On my first day teaching the program, I had participated in less than two days of training and was desperately grasping the manual looking for guidance on how to build a classroom that would promote self-regulation in the 25 four- and five-year-olds who were streaming into my classroom. The first section of my training manual was titled "Self-Regulation Games," and the first topic in that section was, "Fingerplays and Clapping Games."

While I had learned a few fingerplays from watching veteran teachers in my building, I really only had one or two that were a regular part of my practice at that point. I loved using them to get my students' attention, but at the time had no idea that the fingerplays were doing so much more. The Tools curriculum gave me so many more fingerplays to use in my classroom and also opened up my eyes to the epistemological science behind them.

The resources I received in that training explained how students who join in a fingerplay are practicing self-regulation by inhibiting some behaviors (such as talking to friends or playing with their shoelaces on the carpet) and acting others (engaging in the prescribed movements). The authors of the curriculum also included ways to make these rhymes more challenging and engaging, such as changing the speed (faster/slower) or changing the tone of voice (softer). The curriculum emphasized that if children are no longer regulating for a certain rhyme, you can make it more challenging by adding in one of these elements or just introducing a new rhyme. In each situation, children are practicing their self-regulation skills by inhibiting specific physical movements and intentionally engaging in one (soft recitation, the desired hand movements, etc.).

This was exactly the information I needed to decide on a new rhyme on the first day of school. While "Open and Shut Them" had become a staple in my classroom, I decided to try one of the new rhymes I had learned from my training:

> Ten little horses came to town (Hold two hands up)
> Five were black (hold up hand, showing five fingers)
> Five were brown (hold up other hand)
> They galloped up (raise hands in air)
> They galloped down (drop hands down)
> Then they galloped out of town (hands separate and go around)
> Clop-clop, clop-clop, clop-clop, clop-clop...
> (children make a clicking noise with their tongue and pretend to holding the horse's reins)

Throughout the day, as I was teaching the new routines and procedures I had learned in the training, I had this rhyme to return to. We practiced it, and then repeated it getting softer and softer until we were only mouthing the words and making the clicking sound at the end. By doing this, the children took control of their own self-regulation, and instead of me telling them to quiet down, they did it themselves as a part of the rhyme.

That year would be a challenging one for me as I had a lot to learn about the Tools curriculum, while in the process of implementing. However, I learned a great deal about how to promote self-regulation in my students and came to be a huge advocate for the program. Self-regulation is truly the skill that allows students to access the rest of the instructional program, never mind successfully navigating the world outside school. I am forever grateful for learning how to incorporate self-regulatory activities into my practice, starting with the small but mighty fingerplay.

> **Handy Highlights**
>
> ☞ Increased academic demands can come at the expense of time and focus on important social, emotional, and physiological developments of students.
> ☞ In addition to early literacy skills, fingerplays help childhood development in four areas: social skills, fine and gross motor skills, oral language development, and self-regulation.
> ☞ Fingerplays can be a joyful way to integrate more holistic learning and development opportunities into your classroom.

References

American Speech-Language-Hearing Association. (n.d.a). *Speech and language development*. ASHA. https://www.asha.org/public/speech/development/speech-and-language/

American Speech-Language-Hearing Association. (n.d.b). *Speech sound disorders*. ASHA. https://www.asha.org/public/speech/disorders/speech-sound-disorders/

Bodrova, E., & Leong, D. J. (2024). *Tools of the mind: The Vygotskian approach to early childhood education* (3rd ed.). Routledge.

Haidt, J. (2024). *The anxious generation: How the great rewiring of childhood is causing an epidemic of mental illness*. Penguin Random House.

Siegel, D. J., & Bryson, T. P. (2012). *The whole-brain child: 12 revolutionary strategies to nurture your child's developing mind*. Delacorte Press.

Tough, P. (2012). *How children succeed: Grit, curiosity, and the hidden power of character*. Houghton Mifflin Harcourt.

4

In Practice

I hope that, after learning about the benefits of using fingerplays with children, you are eager to start. This chapter will give you the tools you need to do exactly that. While the appendix is full of fingerplays, this chapter will show you what they look like in the context of your work as an educator. I begin with a plan for how to introduce a rhyme to children, and then proceed to explain a number of different times they can be used within an academic day. Finally, I provide suggestions for using them at home or in a childcare setting.

How to Introduce a Fingerplay

Children are spilling into the classroom from recess. Some are still hanging coats in cubbies, others are admiring the acorns they collected from the playground, and some are nursing scrapes from their tumble off the slide. You give a few minutes for some children to move toward the carpet and then you begin:

> I have ten little fingers and they all belong to me (Hold up two hands)
> I can make them do things, would you like to see? (Wiggle fingers on both hands)

I can shut them up tight, or open them wide (Shut tight and open wide along with words)
I can put them all together or make them all hide (Press palms together, put behind your back)
I can make them jump high, I can make them jump low (Reach high and low)
I can fold them all quietly and hold them just so (fold hands together and place in lap)

And just like that, you have completed the first step to using fingerplays in your classroom!
Introducing a new fingerplay follows four simple steps.

1. Model the rhyme and actions: You do not need to provide an introduction or prepare your students in any way. Simply begin the rhyme. Model with enthusiasm and a clear voice, using the hand motions that accompany the rhyme.
2. Repeat with an echo: As soon as you complete the rhyme, you can begin again. Say one line at a time, and ask students to echo the line to you directly after you say it, modeling the accompanying hand motions. Continue one line at a time until you complete the rhyme.
3. All together now: Repeat the rhyme one more time; however, this time, encourage the children to join you, reciting the rhyme chorally.
4. Symbol and practice: After you have completed steps 1–3, you can draw or show students a key image for the rhyme. Using an image to represent the rhyme is helpful for a number of reasons. First, it will help you as the adult remember which rhymes you have already introduced and therefore which you can use when needed. Second, it will provide you with a physical item you can use to prompt students to begin a fingerplay without speaking. This is helpful if you are working with a small group or one student and need to manage the rest of the group. Finally, the image allows

students access to the rhyme even if they cannot write or read all of the words. Students can choose from the introduced rhymes using the images. They can draw images on their own during free choice time and share them with family at home. Chapter 6 has a collection of some favorite fingerplays including an anchor image for each. I even include step-by-step drawing instructions for support!

You can draw the symbol for the rhyme onto an index card, and keep the stack of your index cards with all the rhyme symbols close at hand. Whenever you want to use a finger rhyme, you can pull the card out of your deck and show it to the children. After practicing a few times, they will go right into the rhyme as soon as you show them the symbol.

You can also store your symbols in a three-ring binder or even by placing them on popsicle sticks to hold up to signal the rhyme. Whatever system works best for you!

Let's imagine what the *whole* process would look like in practice.

Students are slowly gathering on the carpet after cleaning up from play centers. Some students are finishing cleaning, some are chatting with friends on the carpet, perhaps others are staring into space, playing with their shoelaces, or doing a hand game with a friend.

You decide to introduce a new rhyme to the students to help collect them together for the next phase of your day.

You begin:

Here is the beehive. Where are the bees?
(Hold one hand out in a fist. Put the other hand and arm up like asking a question)
Hidden away where nobody sees.
(Put the open hand over the fist, covering it)
Watch and you'll see them come out of the hive,
(Keep the fist covered, look at your hands)

One, two, three, four, five.
(Count one finger on one, two fingers on two, etc.)
Bzzzzzz!
(point finger toward students)

All of the children have eyes on you now. While you have their attention you move past step 1 (introduction) and on to step 2, having them repeat the rhyme to you, line by line.
You say:
"Let's try that again, together."

Here is the beehive (*Students repeat while mimicking hand motions*)
Where are the bees? (*Students repeat while mimicking hand motions*)
Hidden away where nobody sees. (*Students repeat while mimicking hand motions*)
Watch and you'll see them come out of the hive (*Students repeat while mimicking hand motions*)
One, two, three, four, five. - Bzzzz! (*Students repeat while mimicking hand motions*)

The children did great. So you move to step 3, doing everything together, rather than the children echoing you:
"Wow, you did such a great job. Let's do it once more at the same time and then I will show you the special symbol for this rhyme."

You and the students repeat the rhyme all together. They do great, again, and you move on to step 4 to introduce the symbol:
"That is a silly one! Now I am going to show you the special symbol for this rhyme. This rhyme is all a beehive, so I am going to draw a beehive. A beehive is a special home where bees live and work together."

You take out an index card and how them how to draw the symbol:
"I start by drawing a small oval shape that will be the top part of our beehive. Next, I draw three ovals getting bigger as they go down. Then I add four more, getting smaller as I go

down. Finally, I add a small circle in the middle of the hive. This is the little door where bees go in and out.

Now, when you see this image you know we can begin. Let's practice once more!"

Show image and repeat the rhyme all together. Add the image to your collection of introduced rhymes. You can store these as index cards in a stack, with a binder ring, in sheet protectors, on popsicle sticks, or any way that works for you and your students.

Routines for Using Fingerplays in the Classroom

While I will provide you with many opportunities to use fingerplays in your classroom, home or childcare setting, please know there is no right or wrong time to use them. Most of the opportunities I will share are included because I experimented with them during my time in the classroom. The rhymes and motions are simply a tool – you are the engineer of your time with children, make them work for you!

Attention Getters

Capturing the students' attention, along with transitions, is probably the most common time for using fingerplays. It was the example I provided in the introduction, when – exhausted and over my head – I wandered by the veteran teacher's classroom and saw her students rapt. There are many times throughout the day when we need (or would like) all of the children to hear what we are about to say. Ensuring that all students are paying attention to us before we start speaking is a great way to prevent confusion or repeating directions again and again. It is also a great way to gather attention from competing interests before beginning a read aloud or a new lesson.

Anyone who has spent time with children knows there is no end to what can take their attention away from the teacher. Their friend is making an interesting noise. Someone is cutting the grass outside. Their shoelaces have untied (again). There is a small bit of play doh under their nails and it absolutely needs to be removed right now. Using a fingerplay in these moments is like using a trump card. Fingerplays are more fun and engaging than (almost) everything else that may be taking our children's attention away from us.

There are a number of ways to get children's attention. Some examples include call and response chants "1-2-3, eyes on me. 1-2 eyes on you!" or "Everybody stop, hands on top!" Some educators use countdowns or ask "if you can hear me, touch your nose." All of these methods can work, but – as a fingerplay enthusiast – I find using action rhymes as an attention getter to be the most effective.

We are competing with a number of (very exciting) things. We want to capture students' attention and using rhyme along with motions helps to draw in students' whole bodies and minds. Just as importantly, it does so in a collaborative way that doesn't demand child compliance. Nor does it hold up some students as "good" if they are simply the first to comply. When you begin a fingerplay, it is simply an invitation for students to join you, but to join you in something that is engaging enough to win them over.

As I outlined in the first section, you do not need to formally introduce the fingerplay or ask students to join you. Just begin with enthusiasm and energetic hands and you will see the students join in. Certain rhymes work better than others as attention getters. I especially like the ones that end with children putting their hands in their laps or down by their sides. This allows you to go *right* into your story, directions, or lesson without competing with students buzzing their fingers around or making clicking noises with their tongues. Some fingerplays that work especially well as attention getters are:

- ♦ Open and Shut Them
- ♦ Grandma's Glasses
- ♦ Ten Little Fingers
- ♦ Two Little Hands
- ♦ Clap Clap Clap

Transitions

There are a lot of transitions in our days. Entering the classroom, sitting for a snack, washing our hands, moving to the carpet, lining up for the hallway... we almost spend as much time transitioning as we do on other parts of the day. And, as someone who works with young children, you know very well that transitions are some of the hardest times. You may be transitioning from a preferred activity to a less preferred activity, or perhaps a child hasn't finished their masterpiece in the art center. Children may be tasked with following a multistep direction, such as retrieving their lunch box, their jacket, and lining up at the door. Consider using action rhymes that may help make them (at least a bit) smoother. Also, remember that homemade rhymes work just as well as ones I have included in this book. Feel free to create your own rhymes and accompanying movements that directly connect to your specific routines and procedures.

Thematic Support

As reviewed in earlier chapters, students who read a book or passage about a topic they have background knowledge of are more likely to understand what they are reading. And this makes sense, doesn't it? Imagine having no familiarity with baseball and reading this short passage:

> *The pitcher fires a fastball inside and the batter turns on it, ripping a line drive down the left-field line. It drops fair and skims into the corner. The left fielder fields it cleanly and throws to the cutoff man as the batter digs for second. The relay to the shortstop is close, but the batter's hand reaches the bag just before the tag—safe at second with a double.*

If you are a baseball fan, you probably have a pretty clear picture in your mind about what that passage is illustrating. However, if the only sport your family has ever watched or played is soccer, this is likely gibberish to you. Since we know how important a wide range of content is for successful book and media understanding, more and more schools are moving to curriculum structured around content specific themes. This allows children to become experts in a content area and to develop a collection of vocabulary words that are connected and rooted in meaning.

As I discussed in Chapter 2, I will not pretend that using fingerplays will provide children with deep content knowledge and better prepare them for complicated reading comprehension down the road. However, fingerplays can play an important role in helping your classroom themes come to life. While we as educators are often aware of our current unit theme or focus in our curriculum, and how the activities we are doing contribute to that curriculum, from the perspective of the children it may seem like we are just reading another story. Using fingerplays that connect to the current unit of study help add depth to the unit and expand the reach of the theme. They can also offer students a more interactive way to engage with certain topics and additional practice with thematic vocabulary.

For example, if you use "Here is the beehive" during a unit on insects, you are providing students with additional opportunities to produce the word "hive" and practice using it with meaning. Again, I recognize this will not be the most impactful knowledge building tool, but it can help your classroom's current theme or unit focus feel more tangible.

Besides the beehive example, you can find additional themes and corresponding fingerplays in the following chapter and the resources suggested at the end. Again, you should feel free to make up a rhyme and actions that correspond with whatever thematic unit you are using. You can also use AI to generate corresponding rhymes with a prompt like "give me a simple rhyme and corresponding actions for a kindergartener about _____."

Waiting Times

Perhaps my favorite time to use fingerplays is during waiting times. While we hope that we move through our days using all our time purposefully, there are inevitably moments when we find ourselves with a large group of children who are simply expected to... wait. Maybe they are waiting to board the school bus or to be let back inside after recess. Maybe you are at an assembly and waiting for the program to begin and have a group of children who decide to entertain themselves in less than appropriate ways. You can fall back on well-known fingerplays during these times, even without making a nose. Simply begin the actions associated with the rhymes and watch the students join in. Alternatively, you can bring around a few cards and display them to prompt students to begin.

There are even times when children are left to wait on their own. There may be an emergency with one student, or another adult needs your attention while students are gathered together. You can choose one student to choose a rhyme and direct the others. When they finish, they can choose another student to do the same. This routine allows students to stay engaged and self-managed even without you present. Students can choose from the images for each rhyme or just begin the rhymes that they can remember.

Family Connection and Use at Home

As educators, we are always looking for meaningful ways to make connections between the work we do in the classroom and our children's home lives. Traditional homework assignments like worksheets do not always offer meaningful practice, especially in early childhood classrooms where children are still learning the basics of our written language. However, using fingerplays and action rhymes as a bridge between the home and the classroom can provide students with the opportunity to demonstrate ownership over their learning.

When I taught kindergarten, I was required to send home homework. I have a lot of strong feelings about homework in early childhood, but as a newer teacher I wasn't prepared to fight against this expectation. Instead, I tried to think of how I could use homework for something I did believe in: intentional family engagement. I was lucky to be working in a district that invested deeply in family engagement. I was trained on (and paid for!) home visits that focused on relationship building. We learned how to design data meetings to supplement traditional parent teacher conferences in a way that would help our families understand specific skills and how parents could support those skills at home. And I was fortunate to work with incredible families who truly wanted to do everything they could to support their young children.

As early childhood educators, we bear a great responsibility to shape our families' expectations for what it means to engage with the schools. We never know where our student's families have come from – it is possible that schools were not a safe, enjoyable, or welcoming space for them when they were students. It is possible that they come from cultures that do not expect parents to be involved in their child's education, putting complete faith in the teacher alone to monitor academic growth. It is a privilege to be one of the first faces families meet as they usher their child through their schooling experience, and one that we should not take lightly.

Because of this, it is important that we are intentional with how we ask families for support. There is not a lot of time between school dismissal and bedtime, and much of that time is full of physical self-care tasks like dinner and bath. As early childhood educators, we know the importance of unstructured and child-led play time, as well as opportunities for gross motor movement and play. I would much prefer a family member to bring their child to the neighborhood park for 30 minutes, rather than sit down and force them to work through an addition and subtraction worksheet.

Given all of these considerations, I worked with my colleagues to create a homework practice that went beyond sending home worksheets. We thought about our priorities when it came to family engagement. We wanted families to know what we were working on in school (since we all know how children can remember so little from their day). We thought of meaningful ways that students could practice the most important foundational skills, both to become more fluent in those skills but also as a way of showing families *how* we practiced these skills. For example, instead of just telling them that we were working on initial sound identification, we would explain how to play an "I spy" game that focused on isolating initial sounds ("I spy with my little eye something that begins with the sound/t/… yes a teapot!"). You can see an example of a homework page in Figure 4.1.

As you can see, fingerplays are one of the different things we ask students to "practice" with their families. In addition to including it on weekly homework assignments, I like to share the concept of fingerplays with families and encourage them to play with language in other ways at home.

Essentially, I would share with them an overview of what Chapter 2 explains: the way students learn to read is through the sound paths in their brain. The more comfortable children are with the different sounds and how they change and work together, the smoother their path to reading will be. And also, it is fun! My goal is for families to know that they have the knowledge and creativity to play with language on their own. I love hearing how families take what we start together in school and make it their own.

> A peanut sat on a railroad track, (tap fingers together making an X)
> His heart was all aflutter, (tap heart)
> Around the bend (put palms together and mime going around a curve)
> came train number 10, (put up all ten fingers)
> Uh Oh! Peanut Butter! (Palms on cheeks)
> Smash! (clap)

After teaching the children this rhyme and practicing it in school, one of the kids came back the next day and couldn't wait to tell me what his family came up with at home. He hastily

Example of Weekly Homework

Day	Do	Share	Read	Practice
M	Play I Spy with someone in your family. "I Spy something that begins with the sounds /t/"	What did you learn about reptiles today?	A book that makes you laugh. What did you read? _____	Here is the Beehive Rhyme
T	Go on a shape hunt! Find a circle, square, rectangle and triangle in your home.	What do you want to learn about reptiles?	Anything you'd like! What did you read? _____	Saying your address 5 times
W	Teach your family how to play "I have Who has" and play with your word cards.	What is your favorite reptile that we learned about in class today?	A book with a family member. What did you read? _____	Count by 10s to 100.
T	Go outside and play! You can pretend you are a reptile and need to find food for your baby.	Who did you play with at recess today? What did you play?	Anything you'd like! What did you read? _____	Open and Shut Them Rhyme 

In class this week we are...

★ Researching different reptiles and learning about their shared characteristics
★ Learning about different word patterns and how to use them in our reading and writing
★ Working on identifying 2D and 3D shapes
★ Working on separating the sounds I hear in words
★ Counting by 10s and 1s to 100

FIGURE 4.1 An Example of a Weekly Homework Assignment

threw his jacket and backpack into his cubby and ran to me, hands already moving and with a huge smile on his face.

He began:

An avocado sat on the railroad track
Feeling kind of holey,
Around the bend came train number ten,
Uh oh! Guacamole!
Smash!

By the time he had finished, he was hysterically laughing and there were two kids beside him asking to learn. That began a morning meeting focused on what other foods can be smashed up to turn into other things, and what words we could find that rhymed. There were a lot of apples and pears feeling "loose" before they were turned into "juice" and everyone was thrilled. Other students have come into class wanting to share rhymes that their family uses, or maybe songs that are special to them. I love how sharing fingerplays with families opens a door for sharing carrying rhymes back and forth from school. Nothing makes me happier than when a younger sibling comes to me and already knows some of the rhymes I teach because their older sibling brought them home.

Finally, you can consider how you share the fingerplay symbols and words with families. In the past, I have printed the rhymes and corresponding symbols on half sheets of paper and stapled them together as a book for children to bring home. I let them illustrate a front cover and encourage them to put a sticker on the rhymes they like the best. It can be something you add on to as the year goes on, or you can create a few throughout the year. Students love making "mini books" by folding the paper according to the instructions in Figure 4.2. They can choose which of the rhymes they want to include and draw the icons themselves.

No matter how you choose to share fingerplays with the families of your students, keep the mood light and fun. You do not want fingerplays to become something you test or require. Their

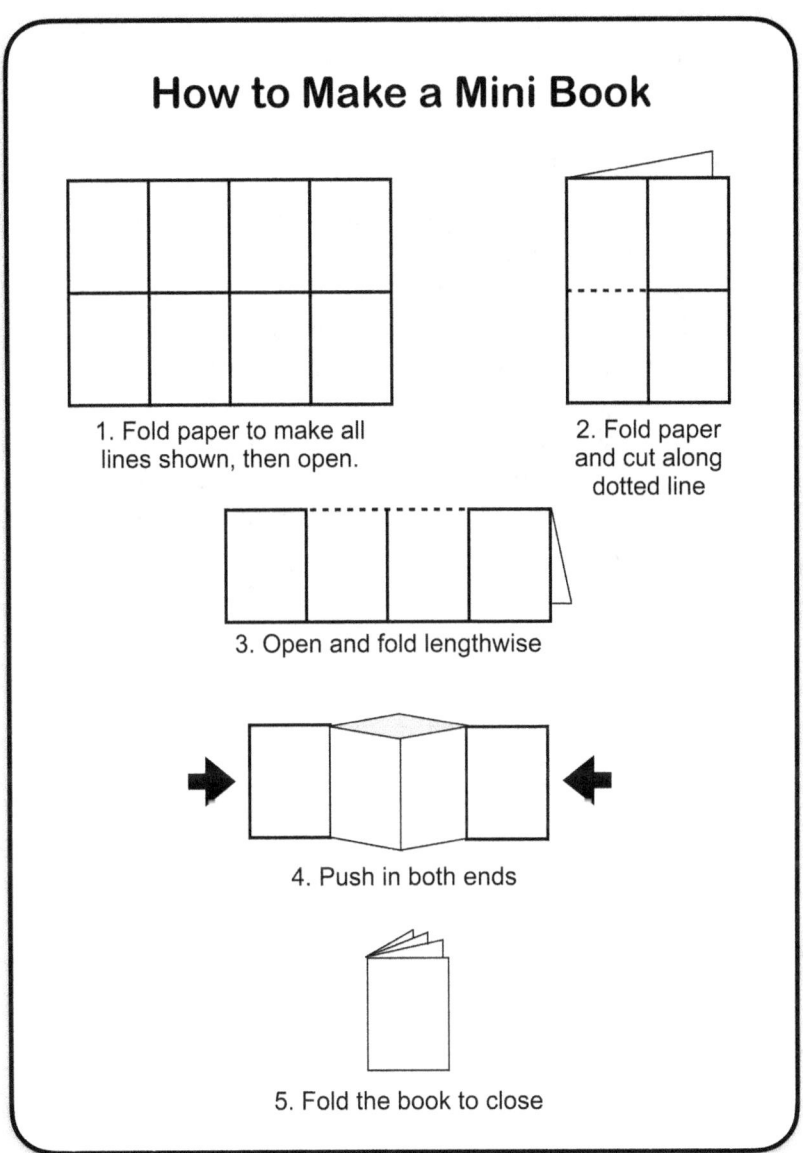

FIGURE 4.2 How to Make a Mini Book

beauty lies in their informality and should remain something that feels fun to share and use together.

> **Handy Highlights**
> - ☞ You do not need to formally introduce a fingerplay. Just start, and the students will join in!
> - ☞ Fingerplays are great anytime but can be most helpful during these times of the day: to get the students' attention, to support transitions, to augment a lesson thematically, and during waiting times.
> - ☞ Fingerplays can also be used at home or in a childcare setting as a bridge to the classroom, providing students with the opportunity to demonstrate ownership over their learning.

5

Rhyming with Language Learners

According to the National Center for Education Statistics (2024), the percentage of public school students in the United States who were English language learners was 10.6%, or 5.3 million students, in the fall of 2021. English language learners are also known as emergent bilinguals or multilingual learners (MLLs), which recognizes that these students come with other language skills. This chapter will refer to students who are learning the English language as MLLs. While the number of MLLs varies significantly from state to state, there is a staggering number of students in our country's public schools who are still learning to speak English. The goal of this chapter is to summarize some of the research about teaching language and literacy to English language learners and to describe how fingerplays can support both language and reading acquisition for these students.

In Chapter 2, we reviewed the recommendations for teaching literacy made by the National Reading Panel. While this panel reviewed a great deal of research on reading acquisition, it did not include research on reading acquisition for students whose first language is not the same as the language spoken in their school. As the number of MLLs continued to increase in the United States, it became clear that there was a need for a similar research review and recommendations regarding reading acquisition for this growing population. SRI International and the Center for Applied Linguistics were awarded a contract in 2001 to establish the National Literacy Panel (NLP). The goal of this

DOI: 10.4324/9781003599746-6

panel was to review the research on the development of literacy among MLLs and to publish a report synthesizing the research to guide practice and policy.

This panel concluded their work in 2006, publishing their report *Developing Literacy in Second-Language Learners*. They found several key points about how MLLs acquire literacy in a new language. First, the panel found that the same five "pillars" of literacy instruction – phonemic awareness, phonics, fluency, comprehension, and vocabulary – are still essential for students who are learning English. Another finding emphasized, however, that these five areas are not sufficient for MLLs. In addition to intentional instruction in these areas, MLLs also need robust opportunities for oral language proficiency.

As we examined in the first chapter of this book, sound is the anchor for reading. As students are able to increase their oral language proficiency in English, they are better able to connect these skills to reading and writing. MLLs need opportunities to practice speaking in English, while also learning the structure of the language for literacy acquisition. The panel also encouraged some adjustment to the five pillars of instruction, including a focus on sounds in English that are unfamiliar to students.

Another finding was that building literacy proficiency in a native language can help facilitate a smoother transition when learning literacy in a new language. This is an important finding, because it emphasized the power of our student's native language. MLLs should continue to speak, listen to stories, practice reading, and participate in rhymes and songs in their native language. As we established the power of these practices for native English learners when learning to read, these practices will support literacy acquisition in all languages.

In her book *Literacy Foundations for English Learners* (2020), Elena Cárdenas-Hagan provides an in-depth look at the ways that English learners diverge from native English speakers when it comes to reading acquisition. While research suggests that phonological awareness skills can transfer from a native language to a new language, there are some instances of negative transfer due to differences in the sounds in each language.

For example, the Spanish language does not have the /z/ sound. As a result, it is common for those students who speak Spanish as a native language to substitute /s/ for /z/. Similarly, they may provide the trilled sound /rr/ for the English sound /r/. In the United States, 76.4% of English learners spoke Spanish as a native language (NCES, 2024). While Spanish and English are both alphabetic languages, the Spanish language is a collection of 23 phonemes, while the English language consists of 44 (Cárdenas-Hagan, 2020). While the common sounds can be building blocks for language learners, teachers must be aware of these differences to help build exposure and recognition of these new sounds.

Cárdenas-Hagan offers specific suggestions for how to tailor instruction in the other components of literacy instruction for students who are learning English, highlighting that literacy acquisition hinges on sound processing and emphasizing the importance of oral language acquisition as a foundation for reading. One of these suggestions is the incorporation of copious speaking and listening opportunities in addition to reading and writing. She suggests focusing on both social and academic language and creating space for students to practice listening and speaking in meaningful contexts. Additionally, she promotes the use of culturally relevant and engaging materials, as well as intentional integration of the child's native language.

Using Fingerplays with Language Learners

Fingerplays can offer all students a low stakes way to practice language. Of the 44 phonemes in the English language, many will be new to MLLs regardless of their native language. Trying out these new sounds, especially in the context of words or sentences, is challenging and can be intimidating. Because these rhymes are almost always recited chorally, students are able to attempt using new sounds without the fear of others hearing them mispronouncing words. Additionally, the action accompanying the rhymes provides MLLs with a support for understanding what is happening in the rhyme.

Fingerplays are also a great way to help MLLs learn common vocabulary and phrases. Consider the following examples:

> Here are my ears. Here is my nose (point to corresponding body parts)
> Here are my fingers. Here are my toes (point to corresponding body parts)
> Here are my eyes, both open wide (point to eyes and then open hands wide)
> Here is my mouth with white teeth inside (point to mouth, open it)
> Here is my tongue that helps me speak (stick out tongue at the end)
> Here is my chin, and here are my cheeks (point to corresponding body part)
> Here are my hands that help me play (hold hands up and open)
> Here are my feet for walking today (stand and walk in place, point to feet)

Learning basic English vocabulary, such as the names of body parts, is an essential part of teaching English as a new language. Fingerplays can be a great way to supplement vocabulary instruction, building in a natural way for students to practice pronouncing the new words they are learning. By pairing this new vocabulary with actions, such as pointing to corresponding body parts, we are helping them connect the new words with their meanings.

Learning common conversational phrases is another essential component of early language instruction. The following well-known rhyme provides students with many chances to practice the common greeting "how are you?"

> Where is the thumb? (hide both hands behind back)
> Where is the thumb? (keep both hands behind back)
> Here I am (bring one hand in front with thumb pointing up)
> Here I am (bring the other hand to the front with thumb pointing up)
> How are you today, friend? (bend one thumb in rhythm with the words, making it seem like it is talking)

Very well I thank you (bend the other thumb in rhythm with the words, making it seem like it is talking)
Run away (bring one hand back behind back)
Run away (bring other hand back behind back)

You can modify the greeting and response to mirror appropriate language depending on the age of the students you are working with. You will notice how this example replaces the traditional "thumbkin" with "the thumb" to make use of more common language. If you want to continue the rhyme, you may consider using family words instead of the names of the fingers (father for thumb, mother for pointer, sister for middle, brother for ring, baby for pinky) as those are more useful words. There are endless ways to modify these rhymes to support your focus.

Fingerplays can also be a great place to incorporate a student's native language in the classroom. Action rhymes are not unique to the English language, and many cultures and languages have traditional rhymes. Encourage students to share fingerplays that they recite at home, or bring in resources that can teach fingerplays in their native language. Sometimes you may even be able to compare the way a similar rhyme goes in two different languages.

La Ocupada Arañita

La ocupada arañita tejió su telaraña vino (touch one finger together at a time, ending with all five fingers touching)
la lluvia y se la llevó (wiggle fingers moving downward, mimicking rain)
Salió el sol Se secó la lluvia (arms above the head, hands touching making a large sun)
Y la ocupada arañita otra vez tejió (touch fingers together again making a web)

The Itsy Bitsy Spider

The itsy bitsy spider climbed up the water spout (alternate finger and thumb touching to climb up)
Down came the rain and washed the spider out (wiggle fingers moving downward, mimicking rain)

Out came the sun and dried up all the rain (arms above the head, hands touching making a large sun)
And the itsy bitsy spider climbed up the spout again (alternate finger and thumb touching to climb up)

Because effective literacy instruction for MLLs is so closely aligned with how monolingual students learn to read, much of the advice given in Chapter 2 is applicable for this population as well. The lessons from the five pillars of literacy instruction still apply to these groups. However, if you are a teacher with a high population of MLLs in your classroom, you can be more intentional in your use of fingerplays to encourage language learning and tailor your lessons to their specific needs.

> **Handy Highlights**
>
> ☞ The same five "pillars" of literacy instruction discussed in Chapter 2 – phonemic awareness, phonics, fluency, comprehension, and vocabulary – are essential for multilingual learners (MLLs) to support literacy comprehension.
> ☞ However, these five areas are not sufficient for MLLs, as they also need robust opportunities for oral language development.
> ☞ Fingerplays can be one tool to offer additional opportunities for oral language practice, supporting students in playing with new sounds and words.

References

August, D., & Shanahan, T. (Eds.). (2006). *Developing literacy in second-language learners: Report of the National Literacy Panel on language-minority children and youth*. National Literacy Panel.

Cárdenas-Hagan, E. (Ed.). (2020). *Literacy foundations for English learners: A comprehensive guide to evidence-based instruction*. Brookes Publishing Company.

National Center for Education Statistics. (2024). English learners in public schools. Condition of education. U.S. Department of Education, Institute of Education Sciences. Retrieved December 10, 2024, from htttps://nces.ed.gov/programs/coe/indicator/cgf

Additional Readings

The Billingual Book of Rhymes, Songs, Stories and Fingerplays: Over 450 Spanish/English Selections by Pam Schiller and Rafael Lara-Alecio

Zero to Three: "Songs, Rhymes, and Fingerplays in English and Spanish." https://www.zerotothree.org/resource/songs-rhymes-and-fingerplays-in-english-and-spanish/

6

The Rhymes

This chapter includes 30 fingerplays. For each, I have included the rhyme, suggested actions and also a suggested image for you to use in your classroom. For each image, I have broken down the steps so help you draw it, or to use with students who may want to draw it. As you will see, the images are very simple. I think there is a power to modeling and drawing simple images in front of children. In an age where "perfect" examples of images are plentiful, children need to see imperfect drawings to help encourage and value their own. Breaking down an image into shapes is helpful, and modeling how to represent something with basic images will help them as they develop as tellers of their own stories. As shared in Chapter 4, these images can be helpful for you to refer to when you are reciting rhymes or to for sharing rhymes with families.

With the rhymes, as well as the images, do not be precious. Don't like a phrase? Change it! Have another idea for an image? Create it. One of the most beautiful characteristics of these fingerplays is their long tradition and how over the years they have been updated, tweaked, and improved on. While researching this book, I ordered a number of collections from a used bookseller online. Inside one of the texts, tucked between the pages, was a collection of three index cards (Figure 6.1).

The Rhymes ◆ 77

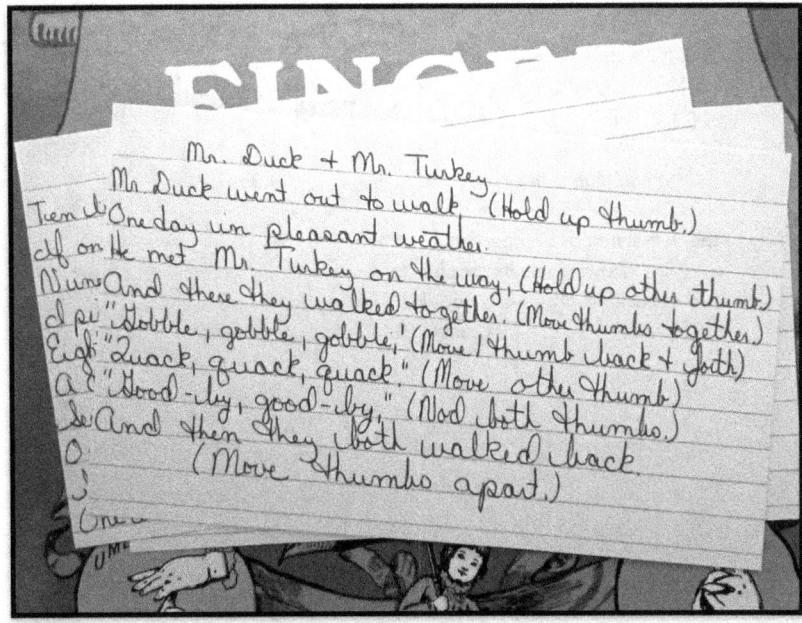

FIGURE 6.1 Index Cards with Transcribed Fingerplays, Found in a Copy of a Used Collection of Rhymes

Source: Photo by the author

I love thinking of this teacher, carefully transcribing these fingerplays to use with her students. Maybe she was new to teaching and, like I did, witnessed their power from the doorway of a neighboring classroom. Maybe a teacher had passed her a book and encouraged her to find time for them in her day. Regardless, this teacher found the magic in this tradition. And I am sure her students were better readers, and lovers of words, because of it (Figures 6.2–6.31).

Apple Tree

Way up high in the apple tree *(Point up high with one finger)*
Two little apples smile at me *(Put up two fingers and point at smile)*
I shook that tree as hard as I could *(Pretend to shake the tree)*
Down came the apples *(Shake hands moving down)*
Mmmmmm, they were good! *(Rub your belly)*
Crunch! *(Mime eating an apple)*

Follow these steps to draw the key image for this rhyme

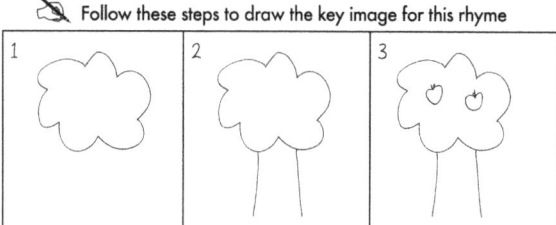

FIGURE 6.2 Apple Tree

Open and Shut Them

Open and shut them *(Open and shut both hands)*
Open and shut them *(Open and shut both hands)*
Give a little clap clap clap *(Clap hands three times)*
Open and shut them *(Open and shut both hands)*
Open and shut them *(Open and shut both hands)*
Lay them in your lap lap lap *(Clasp hands. and put in lap)*
Creep them, creep them *(Walk two fingers from torso to head)*
Slowly creep them *(Walk fingers up to the chin)*
Right up to your chin *(Open the mouth, leave fingers on chin)*
Open wide your little mouth but... *(Quickly bring hands back to lap)*
do not let them in!

Follow these steps to draw the key image for this rhyme

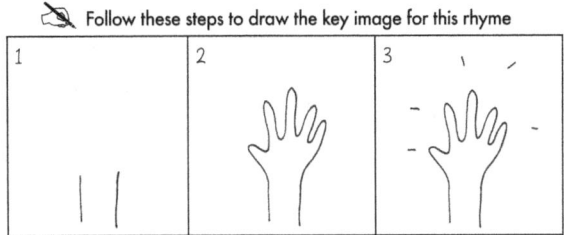

FIGURE 6.3 Open and Shut Them

Here is the Beehive

Here is the beehive *(Hold out a closed fist)*
Where are the bees? *(Hold up other arm like a question)*
Hidden away where nobody sees *(Cover the fist with your other hand)*
Watch and you'll see them *(Look at the covered fist)*
come out of the hive,
One, two, three, four, five. *(Open the fist one finger at a time)*
Bzzzzzz! *(Make your fingers fly around)*

 Follow these steps to draw the key image for this rhyme

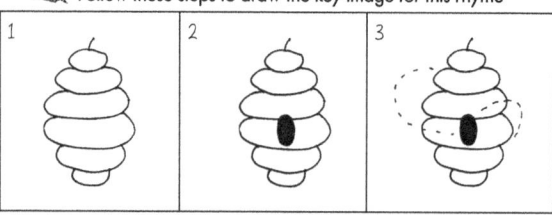

FIGURE 6.4 Here is the Beehive

Ten Little Fingers

I have ten little fingers   *(Hold up ten fingers)*
and they all belong to me   *(Point to chest with thumbs)*
I can make them do things,   *(Wiggle fingers)*
would you like to see?
I can shut them up tight,   *(Shut fingers into fists)*
or open them wide   *(Open fingers wide)*
I can put them all together   *(Bring hands together and hold them)*
or make them all hide   *(Hide hands behind back)*
I can make them jump high,   *(Lift both hands high in the air)*
I can make them jump low   *(Bring hands back down)*
I can fold them all quietly   *(Fold hands in lap)*
and hold them just so

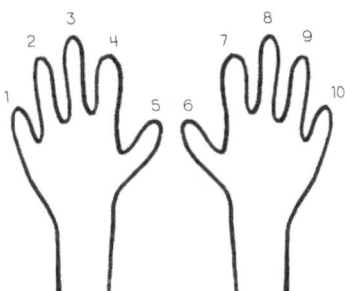

Follow these steps to draw the key image for this rhyme

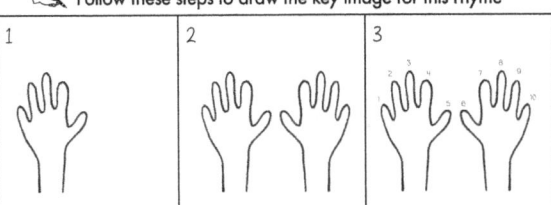

FIGURE 6.5 Ten Little Fingers

FIGURE 6.6 Pancakes

Pitter Patter

Pitter-pat, pitter-pat (Wiggle fingers and move down)
The rain goes on for hours (Tap a pretend watch on your wrist)
And though it keeps me in the house (Put hands above your head pointing hands together like a triangle)
It's very good for flowers (Wiggle fingers pointing them up)

Follow these steps to draw the key image for this rhyme

FIGURE 6.7 Pitter Patter

Grandma's Glasses

These are Grandma's glasses *(Make glasses with fingers)*
This is Grandma's hat *(Place hands on top of your head)*
Here's the way she folds her hands *(Fold hands together)*
And lays them in her lap *(And place them in your lap)*

These are Grandpa's glasses *(Make glasses with fingers)*
This is Grandpa's hat *(Place hands on top of your head)*
This is how he folds his arms *(Fold arms across your chest)*
And takes a little nap *(Close eyes and nod head down)*

Follow these steps to draw the key image for this rhyme

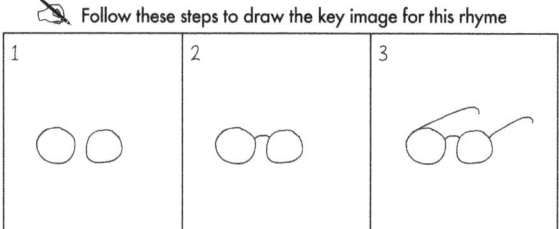

FIGURE 6.8 Grandma's Glasses

Cup of Tea

Here's a cup *(Hold one hand up to the right)*
and here's a cup *(Hold the other hand up to the left)*
And here's a pot of tea *(Put hands together in front)*
Pour a cup *(Pretend to pour a cup on the right)*
And pour a cup *(Pretend to pour a cup on the left)*
And have a sip with me *(Sip a pretend cup of tea)*

Follow these steps to draw the key image for this rhyme

FIGURE 6.9 Here's a Cup of Tea

Blackbirds

Two little blackbirds sitting on a hill *(Hold up one finger on each hand)*
One named Jack *(Make a beak with each hand, open*
and one named Jill *and close to the beat)*
Fly away Jack, *(Fly one hand behind your back)*
Fly away Jill *(Fly other hand behind your back)*
Come back Jack, *(Bring back one hand)*
Come back Jill *(Bring back other hand)*

📝 Follow these steps to draw the key image for this rhyme

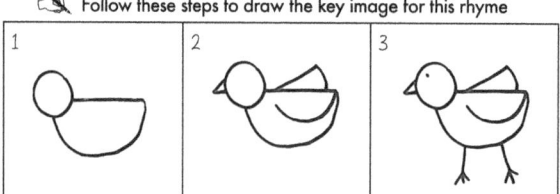

FIGURE 6.10 Blackbirds

Great Big Ball

A great big ball *(Hold hands wide apart)*
A middle-sized ball *(Bring hands closer together)*
And a little ball I see *(Bring hands closer together)*
Let's count them all together... *(Point finger at three different spots)*
One, two, three! *(Hold up one, then two, then three fingers)*

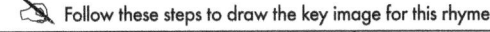
Follow these steps to draw the key image for this rhyme

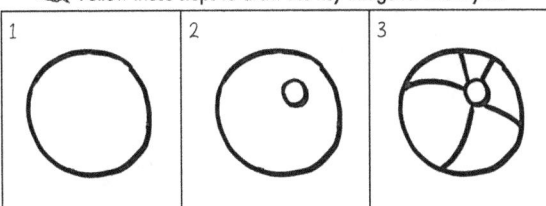

FIGURE 6.11 Great Big Ball

Peanut

A peanut sat on a railroad track *(Tap two fingers against two fingers)*
His heart was all a-flutter *(Tap heart with your hand)*
Around the bend *(Hands together and swerve them*
came train number ten *back and forth)*
Uh oh! Peanut butter! *(Put hands on both cheeks)*
Smash! *(Clap hands together)*

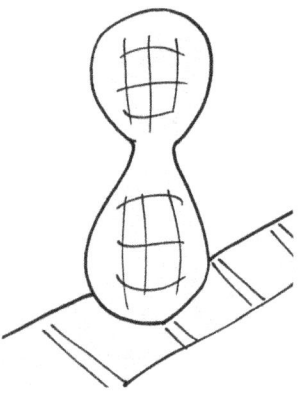

Follow these steps to draw the key image for this rhyme

FIGURE 6.12 Peanut

Elephant

The elephant goes like this and that *(Put hands out one at a time)*
He's oh so big, and he's oh so fat *(Reach arms high, reach arms wide)*
He has no fingers and he has no toes, *(Wave finger side to side)*
But goodness, gracious, what a nose! *(Put arm out in front of face and hang arm down like a trunk)*

 Follow these steps to draw the key image for this rhyme

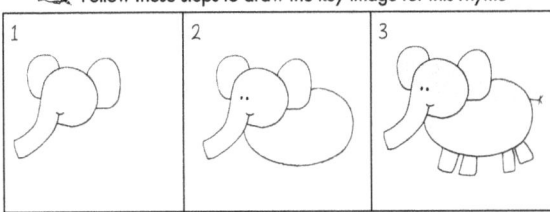

FIGURE 6.13 The Elephant

On My Head

On my head my hands I place *(Place hands on top of head)*
On my shoulders, on my face, *(Touch shoulders and cheeks)*
On my hips and at my side *(Touch hips then arms down at side)*
Then behind me they will hide *(Hold hands behind back)*

Follow these steps to draw the key image for this rhyme

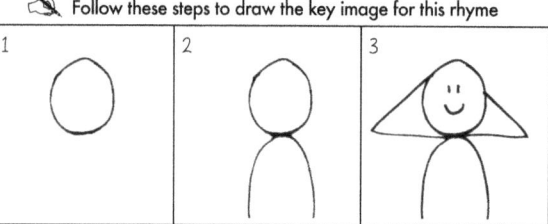

FIGURE 6.14 On My Head

Gray Squirrel

Gray squirrel, gray squirrel *(Standing with hands on hips)*
Swish your bushy tail *(Sway hips)*
Gray squirrel, gray squirrel *(Standing with hands on hips)*
Swish your bushy tail *(Sway hips)*
Wrinkle up your little nose *(Wrinkle nose)*
Hold a nut between your toes *(Mime holding a nut in hands)*
Gray squirrel, gray squirrel *(Standing with hands on hips)*
Swish your bushy tail *(Sway hips)*

Follow these steps to draw the key image for this rhyme

FIGURE 6.15 Gray Squirrel

Popcorn

I'm a piece of popcorn, *(Point thumbs to chest)*
put me in a pan *(Jump forward)*
Shake me, shake me *(Shake arms and legs)*
as fast as you can
As the flame gets bigger *(Wiggle fingers like a flame)*
and hot hot hot
Watch me carefully *(Bend down to the ground)*
Cause I will POP! *(Jump up)*

Follow these steps to draw the key image for this rhyme

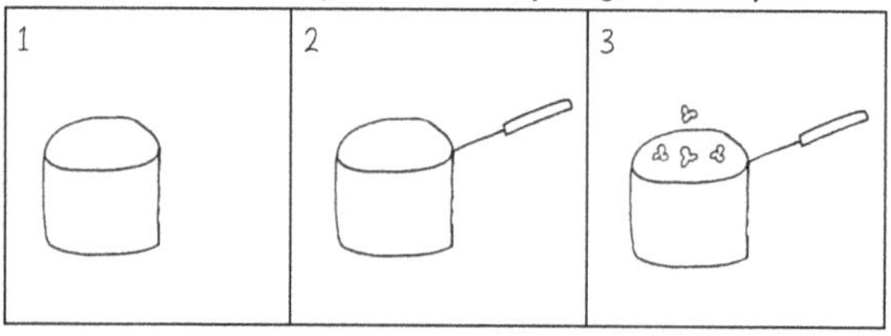

FIGURE 6.16 Popcorn

Jack In The Box

Jack-in-the-box *(Bend down, holding your knees)*
still as a mouse *(Stay still in that position)*
deep down inside
your small little house
Jack-in-the-box
resting so still *(Place head down on knees)*
Won't you come out? *(Shake head slowly "no")*
... *(Stay still until the...)*
Yes, I will! *(pop up with a smile)*

Follow these steps to draw the key image for this rhyme

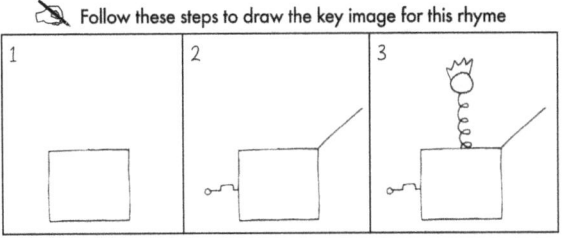

FIGURE 6.17 Jack-in-the-Box

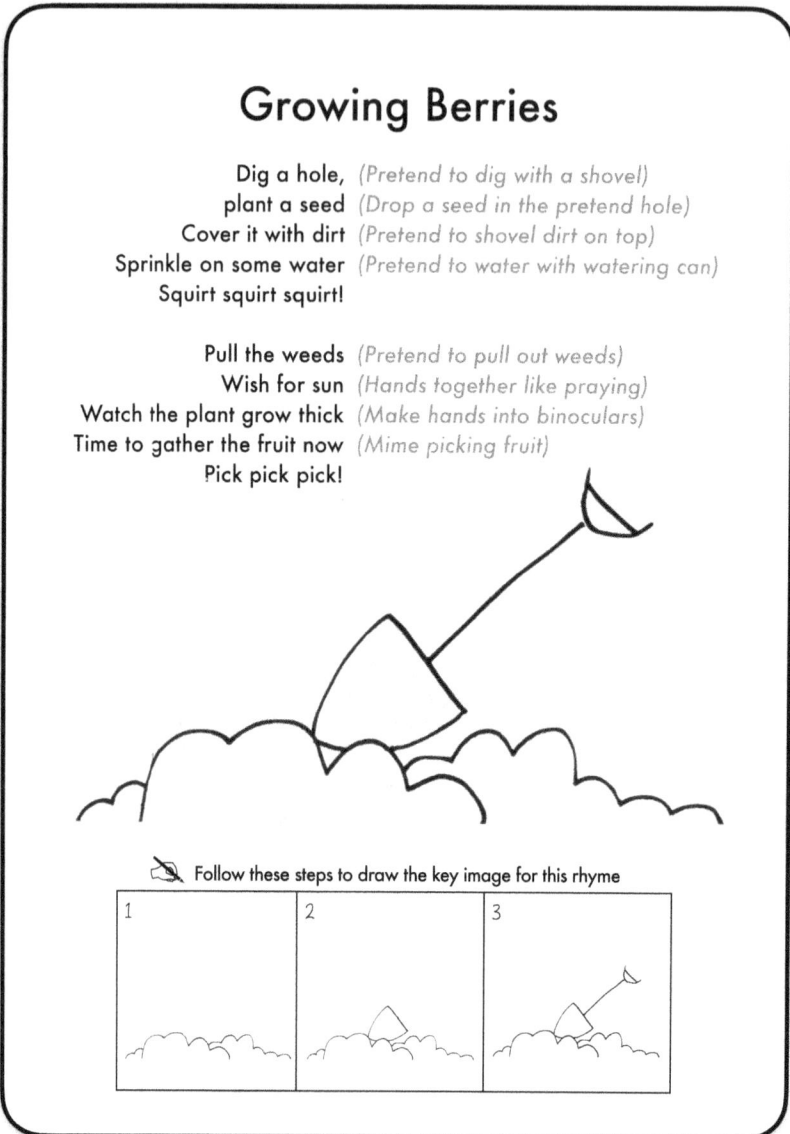

FIGURE 6.18 Growing Berries

Zoom Zoom Zoom

Zoom, zoom, zoom *(Hands together and side to side)*
We're going to the moon *(Put hands up towards the sky)*
If you want to take a trip *(Wag finger forward)*
Climb aboard my rocket ship *(Pretend to water with watering can)*
Zoom, zoom, zoom *(Hands together and side to side)*
We're going to the moon *(Put hands up towards the sky)*

Follow these steps to draw the key image for this rhyme

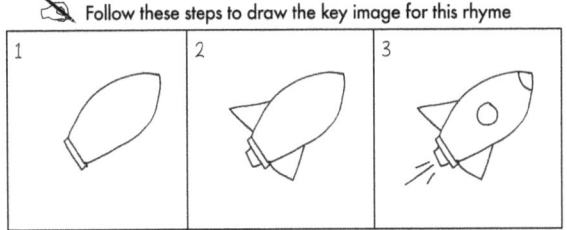

FIGURE 6.19 Zoom Zoom Zoom

Falling Leaves

All the leaves are falling down *(Flutter hands downwards)*
Orange, green, red and brown *(Point to four different spots)*
Listen closely, hear them say *(Cup hands around ears)*
Wintertime is on its way *(Cup hands around mouth, whisper)*

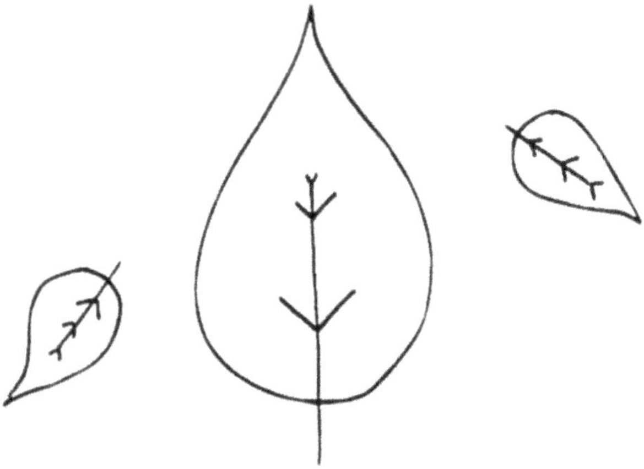

Follow these steps to draw the key image for this rhyme

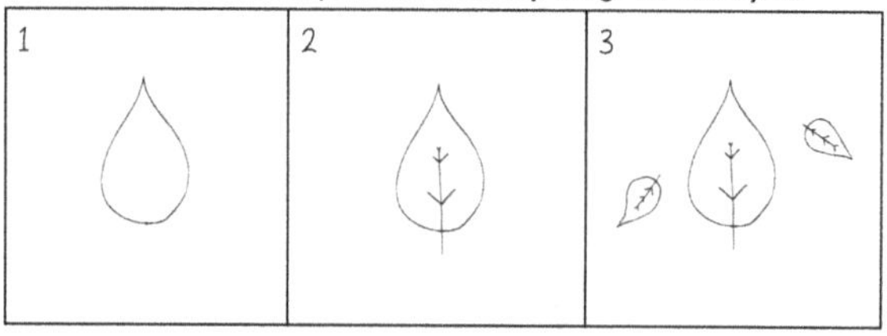

| 1 | 2 | 3 |

FIGURE 6.20 Falling Leaves

Sleepy Caterpillars

"Let's go to sleep" *(Place palms together*
the caterpillar said *under side of head)*
As it tucked itself *(Make a fist and wrap*
into its chrysalis beds *the other hand around it)*
It will awaken by and by *(Slowly unfold and hold up fingers)*
And slowly emerge as a butterfly *(Link thumbs and make hands fly)*

✍ Follow these steps to draw the key image for this rhyme

FIGURE 6.21 Sleepy Caterpillars

I Stand up Tall

I stand up tall and turn around *(Stand up and turn around)*
And jump, jump, jump *(Jump three times)*
I stand up tall and clap my hands *(Stand up straight with hands at side)*
thump, thump, thump *(Clap three times)*

I stand up tall and reach up high *(Reach two hands up high)*
Then clap, clap, clap *(Clap three times above head)*
I stand up tall then bend down low *(Bend down towards the ground)*
Then tap, tap, tap *(Tap fingers on the ground)*

Follow these steps to draw the key image for this rhyme

FIGURE 6.22 I Stand up Tall

The Turkey

The turkey is a funny bird *(Shake fingers under your chin)*
His head goes wobble, wobble *(Shake head back and forth)*
and all he says is just one word *(Point one finger up)*
Gobble, gobble, goggle *(Shake hips)*

Follow these steps to draw the key image for this rhyme

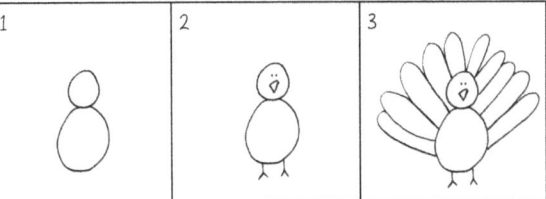

FIGURE 6.23 The Turkey

One Little Body

Two little hands go clap clap clap *(Clap hands three times)*
Two little feet go tap tap tap *(Tap toes on one foot three times)*
Two little hands go thump thump thump *(Hit hands down on the ground)*
Two little feet go jump jump jump *(Jump three times)*
One little body turns around *(Spin around in place)*
One little child sits quietly down *(Sit down)*

Follow these steps to draw the key image for this rhyme

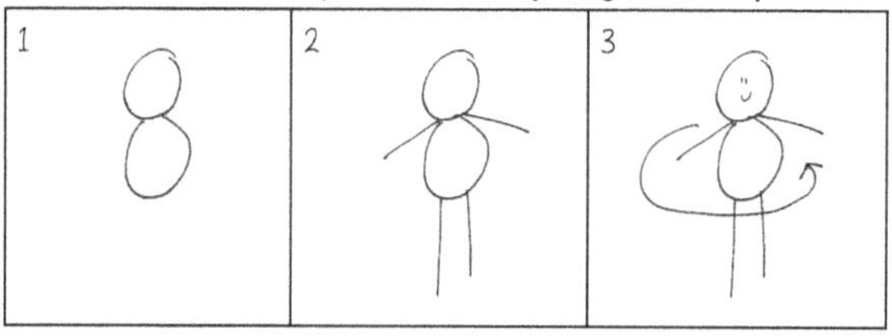

FIGURE 6.24 Two Little Hands

My Garden

Here is my garden *(Hand out and open, palm up)*
I'll rake it with care *(Rake with other hand)*
Then take some seeds *(Hit hands down on the ground)*
and plant them there *(Drop seeds)*
The sun will shine *(Arms touch above head like a sun)*
The rain will fall *(Fingers waving moving down)*
My garden will grow big and tall *(Stretch arms way up and out)*

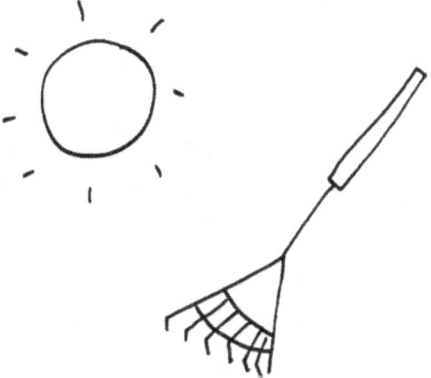

Follow these steps to draw the key image for this rhyme

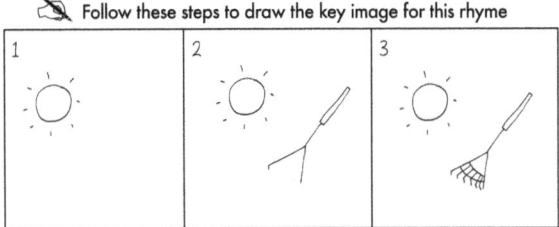

FIGURE 6.25 My Garden

The Snail and the Mouse

Slowly, slowly, very slowly, *(Say this slowly and creep fingers of*
creeps the garden snail *one hand up the other arm)*
Slowly, slowly, very slowly, *(Say this slowly and creep fingers of*
up the wooden rail *the other hand up the other arm)*

Quickly, quickly, very quickly, *(Say this line quickly and move*
goes the little mouse *fingers quickly up the other arm)*
Quickly, quickly, very quickly, *(Say this line quickly and then close*
in his little house! *hands in lap)*

Follow these steps to draw the key image for this rhyme

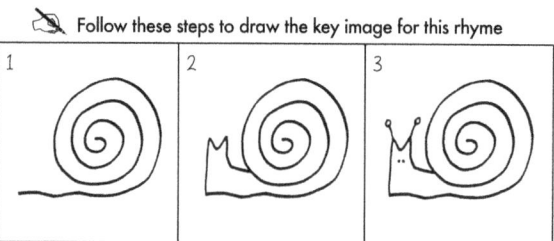

FIGURE 6.26 The Snail and the Mouse

FIGURE 6.27 Ready for the Hall

The Itsy Bitsy Spider

The itsy bitsy spider *(Alternate finger and thumb touching*
Climbed up the water spout *on each hand to climb up)*
Down came the rain *(Wiggle fingers moving downward)*
And washed the spider out *(Cross hands and open them wide)*
Out came the sun *(Two arms above head to make sun)*
And dried up all the rain *(Move arms side to side)*
And the itsy bitsy spider *(Alternate finger and thumb touching*
Climbed up the spout again *on each hand to climb up)*

Follow these steps to draw the key image for this rhyme

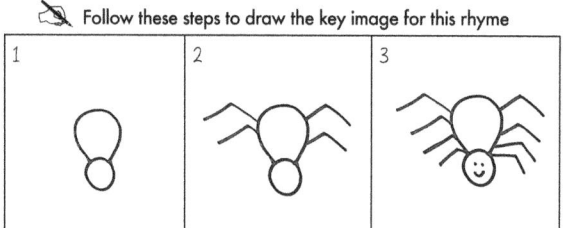

FIGURE 6.28 The Itsy Bitsy Spider

We're Gonna Look

We're gonna look, look *(Tap side of eyes)*
   and listen to the book *(Tap ears)*
We're gonna look, look *(Tap side of eyes)*
   and listen to the book *(Tap ears)*

A mirar, a mirar y escuchar *(Tap side of eyes and then ears)*
A mirar, a mirar y escuchar *(Tap side of eyes and then ears)*

Follow these steps to draw the key image for this rhyme

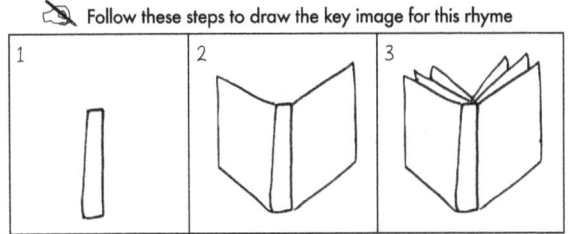

FIGURE 6.29 We're Gonna Look

Little Turtle

There was a little turtle *(Make fist w both hands)*
He lived in a box *(Make a box with both hands)*
He swam in a puddle *(Make swimming motions)*
He climbed on the rocks *(Use fingers to climb up arm)*
He snapped at a mosquito *(Clap hands)*
He snapped at a flea *(Clap hands)*
He snapped at a minnow *(Clap hands)*
He snapped at me *(Clap hands)*
He caught the mosquito *(Grab with hand)*
He caught the flea *(Grab with hand)*
He caught the minnow *(Grab with hand)*
But he didn't catch me *(Shake finger back and forth)*

Follow these steps to draw the key image for this rhyme

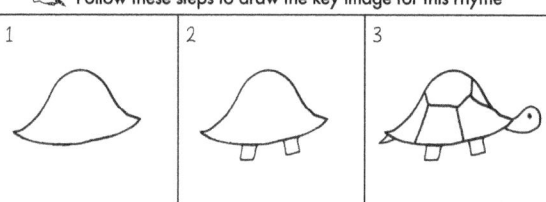

FIGURE 6.30 The Little Turtle

Grow an Apple

Eat an apple *(Bring right hand to mouth)*
Save the core *(Close right hand in fist)*
Plant the seeds *(Bend down touch hand to ground)*
And grow some more *(Extend both arms out)*

Follow these steps to draw the key image for this rhyme

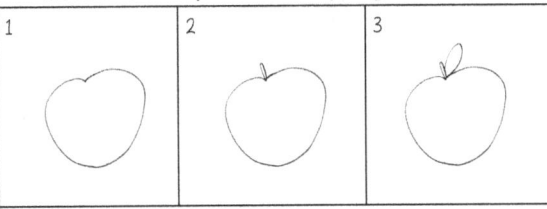

FIGURE 6.31 Grow an Apple

Additional Readings

Children's Counting-Out Rhymes, Fingerplays, Jump-Rope and Bounce-Ball Chants and Other Rhythms: A Comprehensive English-Language Reference by Gloria T. Delamar

Clap Your Hands: Finger Rhymes by Sarah Hayes

Creative Fingerplays & Action Rhymes: An Index and Guide to Their Use by Jeff Defty

Finger Plays for Nursery and Kindergarten by Emilie Poulsson

Finger Rhymes by Marc Brown

Musical Game, Fingerplays, and Rhythmic Activities for Early Childhood by Marian Wirth

Once Upon a Childhood: Fingerplays, Action Rhymes, and Fun Times for the Very Young by Dolores C. Chupela

Preschool Songs & Fingerplays: Building Language Experience Through Rhythm and Movement by Kim Cernek

Songs, Poems, and Fingerplays by Ada Goren and The Mailbox Books Staff

Ten Little Fingers: A Book of Finger Plays by Priscilla Pointer

The Book of FingerPlays & Action Songs: Let's Pretend by John M. Feierabend

The Eentsy, Weentsy Spider: Fingerplays and Action Rhymes by Stephanie Calmenson and Joanna Cole

Too Many Rabbits and Other Fingerplays: About Animals, Nature, Weather, and the Universe by Kay Cooper

For Product Safety Concerns and Information please contact our EU representative GPSR@taylorandfrancis.com
Taylor & Francis Verlag GmbH, Kaufingerstraße 24, 80331 München, Germany

www.ingramcontent.com/pod-product-compliance
Lightning Source LLC
Chambersburg PA
CBHW070404240426
43661CB00056B/2528